DAVID GOWER'S

50 GREATEST CRICKETERS OF ALL TIME

IN ASSOCIATION WITH
TIMPSON

Also available
Geoff Hurst's 50 Greatest Footballers of All Time

DAVID GOWER'S
50 GREATEST CRICKETERS OF ALL TIME

DAVID GOWER

Published in the UK in 2015 by
Icon Books Ltd, Omnibus Business Centre,
39–41 North Road, London N7 9DP
email: info@iconbooks.com
www.iconbooks.com

Sold in the UK, Europe and Asia
by Faber & Faber Ltd, Bloomsbury House,
74–77 Great Russell Street,
London WC1B 3DA or their agents

Distributed in the UK, Europe and Asia
by TBS Ltd, TBS Distribution Centre, Colchester Road,
Frating Green, Colchester CO7 7DW

Distributed in Australia and New Zealand
by Allen & Unwin Pty Ltd,
PO Box 8500, 83 Alexander Street,
Crows Nest, NSW 2065

Distributed in South Africa by
Jonathan Ball, Office B4, The District,
41 Sir Lowry Road, Woodstock 7925

Distributed in India by Penguin Books India,
7th Floor, Infinity Tower – C, DLF Cyber City,
Gurgaon 122002, Haryana

Distributed in Canada by Publishers Group Canada,
76 Stafford Street, Unit 300
Toronto, Ontario M6J 2S1

ISBN: 9781906850883

Images courtesy of the Press Association

Typeset and designed by Simmons Pugh

Printed and bound in the UK by Clays Ltd, St Ives plc

ABOUT THE AUTHOR

David Gower made his mark on the game through the 15 years of his international career from the late 1970s onwards as an elegant and at times prolific left-handed batsman. His finest year came in 1985 when he captained England to victory in the Ashes and in the process set a new record for the most runs in a home Ashes series for an England captain. Sadly not every series as captain reaped quite the same success and he is still waiting for the scars to heal after 'leading' England through two 5–0 defeats at the hands of the all-powerful West Indies teams of the mid-1980s.

David's second career as a broadcaster with, in order, Channel Nine, the BBC and Sky Sports has seen him establish himself as a calm and measured judge of the game. It is with those qualities to the fore that he has turned his mind to picking his 50 all-time greats.

CONTENTS

INTRODUCTION

No one said this was going to be easy. There again, nobody said it was going to be as hard as it turned out to be either. Picking just 50 to be my greatest ever has had me twisting and turning this way and that and not surprisingly the final order (if it really is the final order) was only achieved after numerous revisions, including the late promotion of Kumar Sangakkara after his 11th Test double hundred came just as I was poised to submit the first official draft of this book.

To be blunt, this is the sort of pub quiz-style discussion that I would normally avoid. One of my many failings is that I hate to admit that I am wrong and a list like this will inevitably have you screaming at me, 'How on earth can you have put A, B or C above/below X, Y and Z?'. There will be names that are not even in my list that might be instant selections on yours. That is just how these things work and is all part of the fun, promoting fervent discussion, passionate arguments and agreements to disagree – but hopefully no violence!

I must have had some criteria in mind at the start of the process, although whim and whimsy also played a major part. This might be a game that loves statistics but it is also a game that must rise above those mere facts and figures, and in any case how does one reconcile mere averages across over a hundred years of a constantly evolving sport, one which now sees three clearly different codes in use with Test cricket, one-day internationals and T20? I have no idea how I would have coped with T20 cricket, let alone having to imagine how WG might have played it! Apart from the expansion of those so-called codes, the laws have changed; pitches, equipment, techniques, fitness levels – everything has evolved.

As such, I have tended to give greater weight to what all these extraordinary men have done in what I still like to refer to as 'proper cricket', Test cricket, while at the same time acknowledging the very real and important skills required over 50 overs and 20 overs – hence, for instance, the inclusion of some of the current stars across all three formats, AB de Villiers (another who was granted further promotion, on the back of his record-breaking ODI hundred at the Wanderers in January 2015) probably the most versatile of all.

There are a number of players from my own era of whom I have first-hand experience either as colleagues or opponents, knowledge which, I have to say, made it no easier to happily put them into any order. For instance, I am often asked who was the best, fastest or toughest bowler I ever faced and I quite enjoy giving different answers every time. Well, it keeps me amused anyway – but the underlying point is that one could revise this whole list on a daily basis and never really be right and never really be wrong.

There are those from the current era, some of whom have benefited from the amount of international cricket played today to put thousands of extra runs and hundreds of extra wickets into the record books. One admires both their skill and their determination to play on – none more so than Sachin Tendulkar, against whom I played what seems like several decades ago.

When it comes to those great players from the more distant past, I have obviously had to rely entirely on other sources. Two of the great journalists of my time, John

Woodcock and Christopher Martin-Jenkins, have both compiled their own lists in relatively recent times and both know or knew infinitely more than I about some of these great icons of cricket. Their judgements, other historical sources and, to give credit where it is absolutely due, Simon Wilde, with whom I have collaborated on this project, were all invaluable in helping to assess the merits of men long since dead but whose reputations remain very much alive and whose inclusion in this list was incontrovertible.

I also wondered about knocking 'The Don' off his long-established perch at number 1. Could I, just maybe, put my boyhood hero, Garry Sobers, above Bradman? Garry is my all-rounder to beat all all-rounders – try saying that quickly and often! – who managed to combine a love of playing the game with a love of life in general and a reluctance to head for bed too early that would be challenged only by my long-time friend and colleague in England teams and now the Sky commentary box and studio, Ian Botham. But Bradman's achievements and the story of how he practised his way to the top, beginning with a stump for a bat and a golf ball against the water tank deep in country Australia, could only confirm him as the greatest of all time.

As for the rest, what separates them is probably no more than a decimal point, or in athletics terms no more than the odd hundredth or even thousandth of a second. Please enjoy this book for what it is: a tribute to some absolutely brilliant players, with apologies to those that remain just on the outside – and there are more than a few with excellent claims who will just have to stay on the outside until the next man comes up with his own list of all-time favourites!

I hope there will be amiable discussion to follow, especially when Sir Ian finds out I have placed his arch-rival, Imran Khan, just ahead of him. On that one all I can say is that captaincy swung it for Pakistan's greatest ever cricketer and that the ability to appreciate the finest vintages of Vega Sicilia did not come into it!

Whatever your thoughts, feel free to share them but let me say emphatically this: I am not on Twitter. As far as I know there is at least one relatively sympathetic impersonator out there, who I am sure will be delighted to receive all your comments, adverse or otherwise, and I can only leave him to respond accordingly! The Don, Garry and WG never had to worry about social media and one can only wonder what they might have made of it!

THE 50 GREATEST CRICKETERS

50. ALAN KNOTT

England 1967–81

Alan Knott was one of the purest wicketkeepers there can ever have been. I only played alongside him in a couple of Tests during the 1981 Ashes but saw enough of him over the years, as teammate, opponent or simply observing him on TV, to get the very real sense of a genius at work. His departure for World Series Cricket opened a door into the England team for Bob Taylor, with whom I played many times, and Taylor's own class as a glove-man was itself a clue as to the quality of the man who had been preferred to him year after year. Knott's superior batting played a part in this; as keepers they were both outstanding. It would feel wrong not to include someone in a list of this sort who was a specialist wicketkeeper as opposed to those such as Adam Gilchrist, Kumar Sangakkara and AB de Villiers who, fine keepers though they were or are, were chosen for their sides as much if not more for their batting skills.

Knott had the silkiest of hands. People often say that you only notice a wicketkeeper when he is doing things wrong and on that basis it was easy to overlook how well Knott was doing his job. Keeping wicket standing back to fast bowlers and standing up to the stumps for spinners are very different tasks, but his technique and movement were always excellent. The ball just seemed to nestle into his hands every time he took it. I can remember him taking a catch off quite a thick edge while standing up to a left-

arm spinner, probably Derek Underwood, with whom he formed a great alliance; his hands just seemed to glide into the right position and you were left wondering how on earth he could have reacted so quickly. Very few keepers would have held that catch; most would have seen the ball clatter off their wrist. Keeping does not get any better than that. Taylor ran him pretty close, so I regard myself as very privileged to have played alongside both.

As wicketkeepers sometimes are, Knotty was a complete eccentric, but only bonkers in an endearing rather than an irritating way. Concentrating intently on every ball that is bowled for hour after hour probably encourages a certain quirkiness and fastidiousness; they feel everything must be just right if they are not to commit the inexplicable, costly error. One of Knotty's obsessions was keeping himself ultra-fit, this at a time when fitness was not quite the pre-requisite for England selection that it is now. Like Jack Russell – another member of the wicketkeeping fraternity with oddball tendencies – Knotty looked a bit of a shambles in his beloved floppy white hat, but you hardly cared about that when the ball went so precisely and regularly into the gloves.

He was born to his work. He established himself as Kent's regular keeper at the age of 18 and having been chosen for his first Test at 21 cemented himself as England's first-choice glove-man within months, excelling on his first winter tour of West Indies under his Kent colleague Colin Cowdrey in 1967–68. England had been through several keepers in the previous couple of years and were grateful for the stability Knott offered. He became a central figure in a highly successful England Test side in the late 1960s and early 1970s, and also helped Kent win multiple championship titles and one-day trophies.

He was also a very gutsy, pugnacious batsman who made a speciality of digging England out of trouble in resourceful, unorthodox fashion. His strengths as a keeper were his strengths as a batsman too. His agility and quick-footedness made him nimble around the crease and therefore difficult to bowl to. His ability to concentrate for long periods and watch the ball closely helped not only when he was standing behind the stumps but when he was in front of them too.

It was a great testament to his batting skills that he coped better than most of England's specialist batsmen with the raw pace of Dennis Lillee and Jeff Thomson in Australia in 1974–75. Only Dennis Amiss scored more runs for England in that series; a defiant century at Adelaide was one of five three-figure scores Knott made in Tests. He may have used unusual methods at times but he would not have scored the runs he did in that series – with no helmet for protection in those days, of course – had he not possessed a fundamentally sound technique. He also took another century off Australia in a famous partnership with Geoff Boycott at Trent Bridge in 1977 when they rescued England from a desperate start that had seen Derek Randall fall victim to Boycott's famously erratic running between the wickets.

In 95 Tests he scored 30 half-centuries in addition to his five hundreds, which suggests an impressive reliability. In later times, keepers were expected to offer more with the bat than they were then, but his Test record of 4,389 runs at an average of 32.75 definitely put him in the all-rounder class for his generation. He finished with what was then a Test record of 269 dismissals, which would have been many more had he not signed up with Kerry Packer and for a rebel tour of South Africa, decisions that meant he appeared in only six Tests after 1977. He was only 35 at the time of his last Test and could easily have kept going for a few years beyond that.

49. JEFF THOMSON

Australia 1972–85

Jeff Thomson was a freak of cricketing nature. In his pomp, he was an exceptional athlete with a suppleness and elasticity of frame enabling him to deliver the ball in a way which, if not unique, was certainly very rare, and mighty effective. Shuffling into a side-on position as he approached the crease, he started with his bowling arm low before it followed a mighty arc from behind his back and over his head. Some people found this made it hard to get a clear sight of the ball but I didn't think that was the main problem. He was just quick, even when I first faced him a couple of years after he was at his peak. His peak, in fact, only lasted a few years before an injury diminished his powers but when he was at the top it was one of the greatest sights in cricket – unless, of course, you were the batsman, in which case you had absolutely no time to appreciate the aesthetics.

I regard myself as having been very lucky to face him when I did. When he was sending shock waves through the game in the mid-1970s, I was old enough to be interested in what was happening, but young enough not to be involved. I watched TV highlights of the 1974–75 Ashes series in Australia in which 'Thommo', with the help of Dennis Lillee at the other end, terrorised England's batsmen and some of those images still burn bright, such as Keith Fletcher being clattered on the St George's badge of his cap and the ball bouncing out to cover. (It also provided what would become one of the great after-dinner stories about David Lloyd's pink Litesome protector being knocked inside out by a ball from Thommo,

with excruciatingly painful consequences for 'Bumble'.) It was awesome to watch and remains awesome to contemplate. Mitchell Johnson created similar mayhem in England's ranks in 2013–14. Their mettle was tested and found wanting, and they had the advantage of wearing helmets. Imagine what it would have been like had they faced Johnson without such protection and you have an idea of what it must have been like facing Thomson circa 1975.

He also had an immense physical and psychological impact on West Indies when they toured Australia the following winter. He took 29 wickets in six Tests against them as opposed to 33 in five against England, which suggests they coped marginally better, but the main difference was that it galvanised them into improvement. It was an especially formative experience for the likes of Clive Lloyd, Viv Richards and Michael Holding. It hardened them to the realities of Test cricket and when West Indies assembled a fearsome pace attack of their own they did not think twice about using it to the full. Lillee and Thomson taught them that much.

No wonder batsmen around the world offered up silent prayers of thanks when Thomson was involved in a collision with a teammate, Alan Turner, in the field during a Test in Adelaide and dislocated his right shoulder. Understandably, he never quite had the same flexibility or power in that shoulder again. He lost pace, it was as simple as that. It was tragic for him, but great news for his opponents, and we in the England camp were duly grateful.

If he was awesome before his injury, he was still very good after it. He took 20 or more wickets in the next three series he played, starting with the tour of England in 1977 when he was left to spearhead the attack on his own, Lillee having joined Kerry Packer. Thommo initially and admirably decided to stay loyal to Establishment cricket and the efforts he put in on Australia's behalf when the team were missing many frontline performers were most impressive. Clive Lloyd said that one of the things the West Indies found most striking about Thomson at his peak was his ability to come back late in the day with the old ball, and still summon up some explosive pace to shake you out of the complacent assumption that you were nicely settled.

That was Thommo to a tee. Even in his second career, he was always full-on, quick enough to keep you on your toes, and always trying his utmost. I first faced him on a 1979–80 tour of Australia in a warm-up match against Queensland, and I can vividly recall the ducking and weaving. He appeared in one Test against us that time but I remember him more on our next tour when he played a much bigger part in Australia's win. Despite not being given the new ball, he took 22 wickets at 18.68 in four matches, which rightly suggests he had intelligence as well as raw pace. Used in short bursts, he remained very dangerous. On one occasion when I was facing Thommo shortly before lunch at Sydney, where he perhaps bowled best of all, I looked behind to see Rod Marsh, the wicketkeeper, with his hand held up by the peak of his cap, suggesting that Thommo bowl a bouncer. I then looked at Thommo, who was by now at the end of his mark, and back at Marsh. It was classic 'I know that he knows that he knows that I know' but now I hadn't a bloody clue whether Thommo would go for the double – or treble – bluff or what! I could have tried ducking well before he got to the crease and released the ball but in the end it faded into a damp squib moment as I ended up leaving a length ball outside the off stump. I can only apologise that the end of the story was not more interesting.

By the time I faced him again during the 1985 Ashes,

when he was recalled to the Test side after a long absence, he was a shadow of his former self and no longer as serious a threat, but the legend of Thommo had long since been established and it won't die as long as the game is played. I will always remember him as someone who was competitive, uncomplicated and bloody good fun.

48. KAPIL DEV

India 1978–94

India have been blessed with many great batsmen and spin bowlers but they have often suffered from a shortage of great fast bowlers and all-rounders. But in Kapil Dev they had one of each. Kapil's pace was in fact never of the express variety (despite his nickname of the 'Haryana Express'): fast-medium rather than fast in his early years, and something less than that later on. But he had seemingly endless reserves of bustling energy, swung the ball, and knew how to take wickets.

Even though he lost some nip towards the end of a long career, his figures remained impressive given the unhelpful bowling conditions in which he was often operating. Only two other fast bowlers have taken 200 Test wickets for India, Zaheer Khan and Javagal Srinath, and both had averages on the top side of 30, whereas Kapil's 434 wickets – which stood as the world record for a few years – cost 29.64 apiece. Of the seven India players to do the Test double of 1,000 runs and 100 wickets, Kapil is the only one who averaged more with bat than ball.

Above all, though, Kapil earned a place in history as the man who captained India to victory in the 1983 World Cup, a result that converted the subcontinent to one-day cricket and astonished pundits who had written off his team as no-hopers before the tournament. By doing his bit as a player – 12 wickets and 303 runs, 175 of which were plundered off Zimbabwe in an afternoon of mayhem at Tunbridge Wells – he instilled the belief in his players that they could go all the way, never more so than in the final when they were defending only 183 against West Indies. He bowled 12 miserly overs and took a running catch on the boundary to dismiss Viv Richards. India cricket being the fickle creature it is, he lost the captaincy within a few months but regained it in 1985 and kept it until India's defence of the World Cup failed at the semi-final stage in 1987.

What also marked him out was his background. Born in Chandigarh and raised in the countryside at a time when most Indian Test cricketers came from middle-class families based in the big cities, he broke the mould.

Of the 'Big Four' Test all-rounders who dominated in the 1980s – Imran Khan, Ian Botham and Richard Hadlee were the others – Kapil was probably the least dangerous bowler. His figures would certainly suggest that. But he was very effective in his early years, making his Test debut at the age of 19 and being instantly at home on the big stage as effortlessly as Botham. Kapil clocked up the 1,000 run–100 wickets double within 15 months of his first game and the 2,000 run–200 wickets double in four and a half years. Kapil was just a prodigious natural talent in everything he did. In those days, he did a lot of twisting and turning in his action, but it got him sideways on and in a position to swing the ball. He needed watching very carefully.

As a batsman, Kapil came closest to matching Botham

for destructive and entertaining hitting. Like Botham, he was far better than the 'slogger' label that some might have attached to someone who so obviously delighted in finding the boundary. He could strike the ball in classical fashion and was sound enough technically to score three hundreds against West Indies pace attacks of various vintages, on one occasion in 1983 seeing off Andy Roberts, Michael Holding, Malcolm Marshall and Joel Garner to make a game safe in Trinidad. In all, he scored eight Test hundreds, two more than Imran.

Quite late in his career, at Port Elizabeth, he halted a rampaging Allan Donald-led South Africa pace attack in its tracks with a superbly measured counter-attacking century, scored almost entirely with the tail for company. When he went in, India were 27 for five, which soon became 31 for six. Of India's eventual 215 all out, Kapil's share was 129.

Kapil made something of a speciality of making light of a crisis. While others fretted, he coolly went about fixing things with some measured blows. The classic example of this, of course, was at Lord's in 1990 in an epic Test, which saw Graham Gooch score a triple century in the first innings and a mere single one in the second, and one of the silkiest hundreds you could ever wish to see from Mohammad Azharuddin. Kapil again found himself batting with the tail as India battled to avoid the follow on. With 24 needed, and the last man in, Kapil came on strike against Eddie Hemmings and spotted an opportunity few others would have contemplated. He struck four straight sixes in four balls down towards the Nursery End, where men in hard hats constructing the Compton and Edrich Stands came under fire, and the job was done. It was fantastic to watch, and very brave. Imagine if he'd got out attempting one of those shots?

Botham gets on very well with him. He loves him because

of their shared passion for golf – Kapil has developed into a phenomenal player and has various business ventures linked to the sport – and their shared approach to cricket. They played the game in the same uninhibited fashion and I think their desire to outdo each other spurred them on. Both were close to their best in 1982 when England and India faced each other for six Tests in India and three in England. In what was a largely turgid series on the subcontinent, both hit hundreds in Kanpur, Kapil batting in sparkling fashion for 116 off 98 balls. Then, in England, he hit 89 off just 55 balls at Lord's – had he reached his hundred it could have been the fastest in Test history to that point – followed by 65 off 55 balls at Old Trafford and 97 off 93 balls at The Oval, where Botham himself scored a pretty rapid double century.

47. KEVIN PIETERSEN

England 2005–14

It would have been easy to omit Kevin Pietersen from this list on the grounds of unreasonable behaviour, but it would also have been most unjust. He has played some of the most extraordinary innings I have witnessed either as player, commentator or spectator, and it is those that I would rather remember than the unseemly way in which his England career was brought to an end.

Pietersen ranks as one of the game's greatest entertainers. When he walked out to bat, you simply had to watch because he was capable of amazing things. He manufactured shots other people had not thought of and found original ways to attack some of the greatest bowlers of all time, those such as Shane Warne, Glenn McGrath, Muttiah Muralitharan and Dale Steyn, whom lesser mortals were simply content to keep out.

In the end, he took more risks than the England management was prepared to tolerate in a team that was struggling (this was one of his 'crimes', though not apparently the only one), but it was the risk-taking that made him such a spellbinding sight. It requires daring and bravery to play the way he did because there are commentators, colleagues and team management all ready to question you if it all goes horribly wrong. To his immense credit, everything he tried in the middle had been thought through and practised in the nets, exhaustively so. It takes guts to keep playing the way he did, and he was only as successful as he was through hard work and careful analysis. He clearly had an unfortunate talent for saying the wrong thing at the wrong time, but when he spoke about the science of batting you were aware of how thoroughly he thought about what he was attempting to do.

Let's be clear, England would not have regained the Ashes in 2005 had it not been for him. Many members of the team contributed to the result, but Pietersen led the way by showing that Warne and McGrath were not invincible. At the time, the sight of someone in an England shirt hitting McGrath back over his head into the Lord's pavilion for six, or repeatedly slog-sweeping Warne over midwicket for six, was a revelation. Batsmen simply did not treat them with that sort of disdain. It showed an extraordinary ability to watch the ball and make contact with it, something his height and reach helped to make possible. With the fate of the series and the Ashes in the balance on the final afternoon of the series at The Oval, his bravura innings of 158 sealed the day for his adopted country and cemented his status as superstar and saviour. To an extent, his later performances were attempts to repeat the heroism of that day. Certainly, he seemed determined to entertain first and think about the consequences later.

Nor would England have won the World Twenty20 in 2010 – their first global one-day trophy – without him. He was the player of the tournament and his destruction of Steyn and Morne Morkel in Bridgetown was a sight to behold. He also scored runs in the final against Australia. His assault on Steyn and Morkel in the Headingley Test two years later was even more astonishing, given that it was a Test match and he would have had to weigh the risks more carefully, not to mention that he was by then at odds with some of his team. Steyn has probably never been treated quite so unceremoniously in a Test.

It is also highly likely that England would not have recovered from 1–0 down in India later that year had he not destroyed India's spinners on a pitch in Mumbai that was tailor-made for them. Several months earlier he had done something similar to Sri Lanka's spinners in their backyard in Colombo. He was a man for a challenge and a man for a big occasion, and these were some of the biggest any batsman could encounter. Far from being afraid of a bowler's reputation, he was stimulated by the challenges the best bowlers posed. His development of the switch-hit was a move designed to counter a spinner such as Murali. Others might have viewed it as a risk; he saw it as simply the logical answer to the problem.

His overall figures – 8,181 Test runs at an average of 47.28 – were not exceptional, merely very good, but then if consistency was what you were after he was not your man. He specialised in match-winning innings and provided plenty

over the years. Even so, he perhaps ought to have done better. By the end of 2008, he had scored 4,039 runs and 15 hundreds in 45 Tests at an average of 50.48, so to only add another eight centuries after that and average 44.53 during the remainder of his career represented underachievement. He was 28 years old by then, and should have been entering his best years. The highs were still very high but they became less frequent and for that must be blamed the loss of the England captaincy and his frustration at not being able to spend more time at the Indian Premier League; for both, he appeared to hold the England management and the ECB responsible.

There was no doubt blame on both sides but Pietersen's history of falling out with various teams points to a common denominator. He appeared to have a serial inability to understand how a sporting team functions. Although there are conflicting stories that have emerged from the England dressing room at this crucial time in his career, for all those that saw him as an inspiration you have to wonder how two decent men in Andrew Strauss and Alastair Cook both judged 'KP' to be dispensable. I can sympathise in that a 'My Way' approach to life can set you apart from your colleagues, but, although they are in essence very different characters, one can see parallels with Geoffrey Boycott, who I observed at close quarters at the start of my career. Geoffrey was not a natural integrator and followed his own rules doggedly when it came to the art of making runs. Pietersen is a very different player, entertainment more his bag than Geoffrey's clinical accumulation, but it is a crying shame that his apparent inability to fit in cost him and the rest of us so much.

46. VIRENDER SEHWAG

India 2001–13

Virender Sehwag changed Test cricket, or least changed perceptions as to what was possible from an opening batsman in Test cricket. With his positive play from the first ball, Sehwag set new benchmarks for those at the top of the order, doing for five-day cricket what Sanath Jayasuriya had done for one-day cricket in the 1990s with his ultra-attacking mindset against the new ball.

Sehwag's strike rate as an opener, a role he occupied in 99 Tests and 170 innings for India, was a remarkable 83.10 runs per 100 balls, a figure all the more impressive as he maintained an average of 50 over this long period. It is not possible to calculate career strike rates for most players before the 1970s but for those for whom it is possible and whose careers are complete only Matthew Hayden and Tillekeratne Dilshan among openers possess strike rates of more than even 60, which gives some idea of just how exceptional Sehwag was. David Warner of Australia, who played his first Test in 2011 and has a strike rate in the 70s, seems like Sehwag to have simply brought to the Test arena a style of play that had already worked for him in limited-overs cricket. Sehwag paved the way that Warner is now following.

The really extraordinary thing about Sehwag, though, was his ability to start out with all guns blazing and still get a really big score. The way he played, you might back him to get a quick 30 and be out, but very often he simply kept going. Even Warner has not so far matched him in this respect. More than half Sehwag's Test centuries – 14 out of

23 to be precise – were in excess of 150 and of those two were converted into triple-centuries and another four into doubles. A high proportion of those innings were scored at around a run per ball. Of the ten fastest double-centuries scored in Test cricket, Sehwag has made five of them. All of which is testimony to his extraordinary eye and his extraordinary self-belief in playing out-of-the-ordinary shots.

There can be no higher praise than that Sehwag managed to steal some of the limelight from Sachin Tendulkar, India's most revered batting champion, who must have sometimes wished he could have played with the same freedom and not worried about the consequences. Sehwag was the first and so far remains the only Indian batsman to score a Test triple century and in 2011 he also took from Tendulkar the record for the highest individual score in a one-day international with 219 off 149 balls against West Indies at Indore. That record was itself subsequently broken by another Indian batsman, Rohit Sharma, in November 2014.

Sehwag, who grew up in a relatively poor area of Delhi, where his coaches attached weights to the back of his bat to make him play straight, never really altered the way he played. He was given his chance in the India Test side at the age of 23 after hitting a one-day century against New Zealand off 69 balls. He had opened the innings on that occasion but started in the Test team in the lower middle order. So immediate was his impact, though, with a flawless hundred off a strong South Africa pace attack at Bloemfontein in his first innings, that by his sixth game he was being asked to open on a tour of England. In his first match he hit 84 off 96 balls; in his second he scored a battling century at Trent Bridge.

Understandably he was more successful in Asia, where the new ball did less and the bounce was less exaggerated than in other parts of the world, but he was good enough to score runs in most conditions. As well as those early hundreds in South Africa and England, he scored 195 in a Test match in Melbourne, all his runs coming before the arrival of the second new ball. The criticism of Asian batsmen is that they tend to be found wanting on pitches with pace and bounce, but this could not really be said of Sehwag, at least not until he struggled on his final tours of South Africa and England.

Some of his innings in Asia were simply stupendous. Three such came in 2008. He scored 319 in Chennai against a South Africa attack that included Dale Steyn, Morne Morkel and Makhaya Ntini, an innings that occupied only 304 balls and included 42 fours and five sixes. Against Muttiah Muralitharan on one of Murali's favourite stamping grounds of Galle, he carried his bat for 201 in an all-out team total of 329. And against England, again at Chennai, a quick-fire 83 off 68 balls launched India on their way to successfully chasing down 387. Tendulkar's century may have completed the job but it was Sehwag who made the chase possible by snatching the initiative from England in the space of one extraordinary session. That was match-winning batting on a special scale because he scored so fast that it took the pressure off those who came later to keep up with the clock. The following year, batting against Sri Lanka (and Murali) in Mumbai, he had reached 285 by the time the second new ball became due (he was out soon after for 293).

Sehwag in full cry was one of the great sights of the modern game.

45. JOEL GARNER

West Indies 1977–87

Just his personal statistics were enough to inspire anxiety at the prospect of facing Joel Garner. At 6ft 8in, few bowlers have stood taller, and with those great big long arms and mighty levers of his, not many grounds had sightscreens big enough to accommodate the top of his bowling arm. Garner was phenomenally accurate, but the one word you had to focus on was 'bounce'. You were always looking at a length ball from him and thinking: 'How high is this going to bounce?' 'High enough' was mostly the answer.

Although he was capable of generating bounce, though, or perhaps precisely because of it, there was great danger in the balls he bowled of fuller length. A lot of his wickets – almost half in Tests, in fact – were bowled or leg-before, the batsmen no doubt worrying about the ball that might threaten the glove or head only to find one homing in on their stumps instead.

Garner was a great purveyor of the yorker, the old sand-shoe crusher or big toe breaker. The yorker is a delivery that modern-day batsmen have found ways to lever to the boundary in one-day cricket but in Garner's day we were happy just to keep it out, whatever the game, whatever the situation. I doubt very much if even today batsmen would be hitting him for six if he got his yorker in.

He was quicker than people thought. If he wound it up, he wasn't far behind Michael Holding and Andy Roberts in pace. That wasn't always his role though. The West Indies bowling was so strong that some of them – and Joel was one

– inevitably had to fulfil roles they would not have done had they been playing in almost any other side. He started his Test career in 1977 but it was not until 1984 that he took the new ball, Clive Lloyd preferring to use him as something of a stock bowler. But once the new ball was his, Garner became even more potent than he had been. Somerset naturally used him differently when he played for them and he helped them win trophies with some explosive bursts.

The first time I faced him in a major encounter was in the World Cup final of 1979. It was not to be my proudest moment. We were decidedly up against it, chasing a big total and already well behind the rate required, and Joel was hardly the man to give you something to play with in that situation. Giving myself room to try and carve one through cover just gave him a sight of my stumps. I was out for nought, bowled, one of five wickets he took in the space of 11 balls as the game sped to its conclusion. Four of us were bowled, the other caught behind.

How to score runs off him was a big puzzle for us as a side. We faced him again a few months later in a one-day series in Australia without making much headway and when we then faced him for the first time in Tests in England the following year his control was incredible. In the first Test he bowled 57.1 overs off which just 74 runs were scored (at a cost of seven wickets); in the second, 39.3 overs for 57 runs (and six wickets). It was some small crumb of comfort to me, having been dropped after the first game, to see that others found him no easier to play. Over the course of the five Tests, he sent down 212.4 overs for 371 runs and 26 wickets.

His metronomic capabilities should not be overstated, however. Every blue moon there might be something you could have a go at. He might sometimes give you something outside off stump you could flail at, or something short you

could try and help over the slips. He played in the Jamaica Test in 1981 in which Graham Gooch and I both scored 150s. It was a quick, bouncy pitch but fortunately it was also true in its bounce. Somehow we found a way on that occasion.

He came into the West Indies side as a stand-in for a home series against Pakistan in 1977 and was an instant success. He took 25 wickets in five matches, although there were tell-tale signs that he still had things to learn. His wickets cost 27.52 each and went at more than three runs an over. These were expensive figures for Joel. Of the 14 series he subsequently played, his average strayed over 23 only four times and his economy rate over three runs per over only twice. He was very, very consistent. He was also a fine catcher around the slips and gully.

He was perhaps fortunate to arrive on the scene just as West Indies were reaching the peak of their collective powers and finish in the late 1980s before the decline in Caribbean cricket had begun. Remarkably, he played in only five defeats in his 58 Test matches (in which he took 259 wickets at an average of just 20.97). A lot of that was down to his reliability but of course he was playing in a side with very few weak links.

To be part of the most feared pace attack of all time almost automatically qualifies you to be one of the great individual bowlers. They were all immensely skilful as well as quick, and all decent men too. As a bloke, Joel was a particularly lovely guy, with those big genial eyes of his and that typically Bajan air of laid-back affability. He was known as 'Big Bird' not just by his own team but by everyone. There was a lot of affection for him, if not for his bowling.

44. HAROLD LARWOOD

England 1926–33

Not many bowlers troubled Don Bradman and fewer still caused him genuine concern. Harold Larwood was one who did. Like the very best express bowlers, there was a lot more to Larwood than extreme pace. In his case, he had one of the most vicious break-backs in the game. 'At times [he] makes the ball come back so much that he is almost unplayable,' said *Wisden* of Larwood when he was still at quite an early stage of his career.

Judging purely by Bradman's scores in his first two series against England, it is not immediately apparent that Larwood caused him much of a problem at all. Larwood was England's match-winner in Bradman's first Test at Brisbane in 1928, taking six for 32 as Australia were skittled for 122 in the first innings and two more in the second, but although he failed twice, Bradman did not get out to him either time. Indeed it was not until the final Test of the 1930 series in England in which Bradman shattered so many records that Larwood actually took his wicket. But what the scorebooks do not reveal is that Larwood and the rest of the England players were convinced he had Bradman caught behind off a short ball before he had scored the first of his 334 runs at Headingley – a snick Larwood said could be heard all over the ground – and that Larwood's short-pitched bowling severely discomfited Bradman during the Oval Test in which he scored 232, hitting him in the chest and on the wrist.

It was this that led directly to Douglas Jardine's adoption of Bodyline tactics in Australia in 1932–33. In Larwood,

Jardine believed he had the means to keep Bradman quiet. Larwood was not quite 5ft 8in in height but with a superb sprinting run-up he was able to generate great pace off the ground while remaining highly accurate. Jardine thought that if Larwood was instructed to bowl like this on the line of Bradman's body, or the body of anyone for that matter, with a packed leg-side field, then run-scoring would be very difficult. And he was proved right: scoring runs off Larwood was very difficult. Bodyline tactics were not in fact adopted on all occasions but Larwood dismissed Bradman four times in the four Tests in which he played, as well as twice more in a warm-up match. Bradman got past 50 only once in those six innings and was bowled three times. It was one of the most sustained periods of success any bowler ever enjoyed against Bradman.

Larwood took 33 wickets in the series before hobbling from the field during the final Test with a foot injury. Although he never bowled as quickly again because of that injury, which forced him to miss most of the 1933 season, he would certainly have played for England again had not MCC been so eager to appease the feelings of the Australians, who felt Bodyline was unacceptable. Ahead of the next series in England in 1934, MCC effectively made it a proviso of his selection that he should apologise for his part in Bodyline and – totally admirably – he refused, insisting he had done nothing wrong. That Larwood's Test career was over before he turned 30 was a personal tragedy but there was something heroic in his refusal to publicly express regret over something in which he felt only pride. His bowling in that series had been astonishingly good and the Australians – Bradman apart perhaps – had no personal issue with Larwood, even those such as Bill Woodfull and Bert Oldfield who were injured by him.

As fast bowlers do, Larwood rose fast. Emerging from a mining community at Nuncargate near Nottingham, he played his first match for Nottinghamshire at the age of 19 and within two years had sealed his Test selection by bowling Jack Hobbs twice in a county match and England captain Arthur Carr, who also happened to be his county captain, during a Test trial. In his second match for England he helped them regain the Ashes with six wickets in a famous victory at The Oval in 1926.

For the next ten years Larwood was a scourge of county players who found the prospect of facing him from one end and the left-armer Bill Voce from the other – Voce was another member of Jardine's Bodyline attack – as perhaps their least comfortable appointments of the summer. Larwood took 80 wickets at 18.43 when Nottinghamshire claimed the championship in 1929 but that was actually one of his more expensive years. He had topped the national bowling averages in 1927 and 1928 with figures of 16.95 and 14.51 and did so again in 1931 and 1932 when his wickets cost only 12.03 and 12.86 respectively. Even as late as 1936, when he took 100 wickets in a season for the eighth and last time, his average was again under 13. These figures bear eloquent testimony to his destructive capabilities, as does the fact that more than half his 1,427 first-class victims were bowled.

The irony of the Larwood story is that in retirement he emigrated to Australia, the place where he had been such a figure of opprobrium, and lived there contentedly while counting former opponents such as Jack Fingleton, Woodfull and Oldfield among his friends. He was belatedly and rightly recognised by his own country with an MBE in 1993 when he was 88 years old.

43. RAY LINDWALL

Australia 1946–60

Ray Lindwall raised the standard for fast bowlers in the ten years after the Second World War. He was a terrific athlete who could have excelled at several other sports had he not chosen cricket and the mechanics of his run-up and delivery were widely admired. Fred Trueman, who, like Richie Benaud (writing in the 1970s), rated Lindwall the finest fast bowler he had seen, described Lindwall's approach to the wicket as the most rhythmical of all.

Genuinely fast bowlers of earlier eras had rarely maintained their speed and menace for long in Test cricket but Lindwall did. No out-and-out quick bowler had previously taken even 100 Test wickets; he not only became the first to 100 wickets but was the first past 200 as well and by the time of his last match in 1960 had 228 to his name (exactly half of them against England). At that time only the fast-medium Alec Bedser of England, with 236, had taken more. Lindwall in full cry was reckoned to be one of the great sights of the era.

His action was not without its impurities. His arm was not as high as it might have been at the point of release but this slinginess helped him make the ball leave the right-hander very late in flight. Trevor Bailey said that he never encountered a genuine fast bowler who moved the ball in the air as much or as late as Lindwall, adding that he was also the most devastating exploiter of the new ball. By way of variation Lindwall brought the ball back in off the seam. Lindwall's 'drag', a method by which bowlers took advantage of the back-foot no-ball rule then in operation (no-balls were measured by where the back foot landed rather than the front foot) to steal some extra distance before release, was controversial but also perfectly common. It gave batsmen less time to react than they have under today's laws – and in Lindwall's case you needed every split second available.

Lindwall was the most feared fast bowler in the world in the later 1940s. With Keith Miller as his new-ball partner, Australia knew they had a combination of bowlers of rare power and menace, and neither of them was reluctant to use the bouncer. They first came together properly in the Ashes series of 1946–47 – they had appeared in one Test before that against New Zealand but did not open the bowling – and Lindwall's seven for 63 in the first innings of the final Test in questionable light was a chilling portent of torments to come. When the sides met again in England 18 months later Lindwall made the new ball count in almost every innings and finished with 27 wickets at just 19.62 apiece, even though he played only a small part in one Test because of a strain. He bowled more than half his victims and when he shattered England's first innings at The Oval with figures of six for 20 – England all out for 52, still their lowest total at home – and followed up with three for 50 in the second, seven of his nine victims had their stumps hit. Bradman's 'Invincibles' won the Test series 4–0 and went through the entire tour unbeaten, Lindwall taking 86 wickets at 15.68 in all matches.

The following year the South Africans prepared for the arrival of Lindwall and Miller by practising against baseball pitchers, although as it turned out Lindwall was not at his fastest because of a groin problem. He still took 12 wickets in the series at 20.66, and claimed another 15 at 22.93 when

England were trounced in Australia in 1950–51. It was then the turn of the West Indians to endure Lindwall and Miller on their own pitches. Lindwall captured 21 wickets to Miller's 20.

So dependable was his action and physique that Lindwall did not have what could be remotely described as a bad series with the ball between making his debut in 1946 and the tour of England in 1953; during that time his average never rose above 23. So accurate was he that even if he did not take wickets he rarely went for runs. He suffered a dip when England regained the Ashes in Australia in 1954–55 but within weeks was back among the wickets in the Caribbean, where he also scored one of his two Test centuries.

Lindwall was a more than useful lower-order batsman although in what was generally a strong and successful side – Australia lost only nine of the 61 Tests in which he appeared – runs were rarely needed from him. The hundred he scored in the third Test of the 1946–47 series at Adelaide made good what was already a strong position, but nevertheless the way he struck the ball was a fair indication of his class; coming off 90 balls, it was at the time the second fastest scored by an Australian.

As a youngster, Lindwall was inspired by watching Harold Larwood bowl at Sydney during the Bodyline series and there was perhaps something similar in their styles. Lindwall was lucky in his mentors. He played his early cricket for the St George club in Sydney under the captaincy of Bill O'Reilly, and Bradman took him under his wing during his first tour to England in 1948.

42. ADAM GILCHRIST

Australia 1999–2008

Adam Gilchrist must be one of the most fearless cricketers of all time. It is all very well swinging the bat seemingly without a care in the world at county or state level, it is quite another to do so when a Test match or even a one-day international hangs in the balance. But all games appeared to come the same to Gilchrist. He played in a very strong Australia team, it is true, and one that was often expected to win with something to spare, but Gilchrist played the same for every team he represented, and in all situations.

If he had an advantage, it was in not starting his Test career until a relatively late stage. He was a few days short of his 28th birthday when he finally got his chance, having been kept waiting for his opportunity by Ian Healy, a fine keeper and capable enough batsman to average 27 in Tests. Gilchrist had spent three years in Australia's one-day team and already made a considerable mark as a destructive opening batsman with several hundreds to his name. He thus arrived conscious that there might be few second chances but also experienced enough to know his own game. In his first match he scored 81 off 88 balls and in his second retrieved a dire situation in spectacular fashion. Australia, set 369 to win, were apparently heading for defeat to Pakistan in Hobart when Gilchrist joined Justin Langer at 126 for five. Cool as you like, the two of them all but took their side home, Langer falling with five runs still needed. Gilchrist finished unbeaten on 149.

Quite a few of Gilchrist's best innings came when Australia

were in difficulties rather than when they already had a big score on the board by the time he strolled out at number 7. He said he enjoyed it more when they were in trouble because it gave him something to work with. Not that he could not drive home good positions either; when he went in at Johannesburg in 2002 Australia weren't in particular difficulty at 293 for five and he proceeded to smash what was then the fastest Test double century on record.

Australia owed their strength to many things but Gilchrist's presence was surely a crucial factor in their dominance around the turn of the century. Australia won an astonishing 73 of the 96 Tests he played between 1999 and 2008 and lost only 11. One of those defeats came when Gilchrist himself, acting as stand-in captain for the injured Steve Waugh, made a rather too adventurous declaration at Headingley in 2001. Gilchrist actually finished on the winning side in each of his first 15 Tests. He also played in three winning World Cup finals in 1999, 2003 and 2007, and contributed runs on each occasion, most dazzlingly at Barbados in 2007 when in a game reduced to 38 overs a side he rattled up 149 off 104 deliveries. Some of his knocks were just unbelievable.

The record of this lean, slightly built left-hander was remarkable and leaves him towering above all other international keeper-batsmen. In Tests he hit 17 hundreds and averaged 47.60, highly impressive figures when it is borne in mind what a toll hours spent behind the stumps takes on mind and body. Most remarkable though was his strike rate of 81.95, which places him second only to Virender Sehwag. He was also the first batsman to hit 100 sixes in Tests. He hit 16 hundreds in one-dayers, in which his strike rate of 96.94 again puts him second only to Sehwag among bona fide batsmen. In that format he stands tenth on the six-hitting list with 149. Needless to say, Gilchrist was a big success when he joined the first wave of players recruited to the Indian Premier League in 2008.

Among Test keepers whose careers are complete, only Andy Flower, who averaged 53.70 but batted in far less explosive fashion, can approach his record. Matt Prior, Les Ames and Kumar Sangakkara are among the few to even average more than 40.

It has been the fate of every international keeper since to be measured against him. Every team searches not just for a competent glove-man but a cricketer who can also bat, and score regular hundreds. Gilchrist set the mark, and others strive to meet it as best they can. In fact, several keepers have done very well without quite adhering to the Gilchrist blueprint of reliable runs delivered with all-out aggression – Prior for England, MS Dhoni for India and Brad Haddin for Australia have all had their moments, while AB de Villiers maintained his batting form amazingly well after temporarily taking over the gloves from Mark Boucher in 2012. But the greats do it time and time again and that is what sets Gilchrist apart.

Gilchrist played his early cricket in New South Wales but with the state already having an established keeper he moved to Western Australia in his early 20s. There, like many batsmen brought up on the hard surfaces in Perth, he developed into a strong cutter and puller of fast bowling. The one team against whom his record was iffy was India, whose spinners Anil Kumble and Harbhajan Singh managed to keep him largely, if not totally, in check. A few fast bowlers, notably Andrew Flintoff bowling at his absolute best in the 2005 Ashes, managed to deny him the room to free his arms by coming round the wicket at him and firing the ball into his body, but it was a plan requiring perfect execution. In the next Ashes series, in Australia in 2006–07, Gilchrist exacted brutal revenge, splattering the English bowling to all parts of Perth in what was then the second fastest Test century of all time.

Gilchrist also developed into a considerable keeper. He had to keep to Shane Warne a lot, so in common with a lot of keepers of the modern era, like Healy and Alec Stewart, he improved himself enormously through necessity, exposure and hard work. Again, he had the advantage of working for the most part with one of the most formidable bowling attacks in history, but in the main his standards were very high. When he retired, he had a record 416 Test dismissals to his name, a pretty impressive haul in only 96 matches. 'Gilly' also played the game in a good spirit and earned a reputation, very unusual in the modern game, of being a 'walker'.

41. KUMAR SANGAKKARA

Sri Lanka 2000–

Kumar Sangakkara is one of the most complete cricketers the game has seen. As a left-handed batsman, he has the technique to score runs in all conditions and all formats and the single-mindedness to be one of the great accumulators. As a wicketkeeper, he has served Sri Lanka with great skill and unwavering commitment in one-day cricket as he did in Tests before giving up the gloves in 2006 to concentrate on his pivotal role at number 3. He repaid his team by raising his Test average from around 40 as a keeper-batsman (which in itself is a figure only a select few can match) to around 70 when he plays as a specialist batsman. As captain, senior player and elder statesman he has set an impeccable example to teammates and the game at large.

He is not only a very versatile cricketer but a grounded one. He comes from a part of the world where politics are inevitably involved in cricket, and where the governments and boards that stand behind the players can be reconstituted at the drop of a hat. In such a potentially volatile environment, it takes a special ability to isolate oneself and focus on doing the things that lead to good performances on the field. Not that he has hid from the realities of the world: he did not spare Sri Lanka's political Establishment when he delivered a forthright Cowdrey Lecture at Lord's in 2011. In fact, his intelligence is evident in everything he does. He is always alert behind the wicket and always thinking with a bat in his hand. You can almost see the planning and the manipulation that goes into his innings, the changes of pace, the changes of tack as he works out what the opposition bowlers are trying to do against him, and what he should do in response.

He is more than just a run-scorer on a grand scale, although he is certainly that. He has made 11 double-centuries in Test cricket (plus scores of 199 not out and 192 twice), more than anyone but Don Bradman himself, and when he made his highest score of 319 he followed up with 105 in the second innings. That was in a match against Bangladesh, off whose bowlers he took two further double-hundreds, and he also helped himself to 270 against a weak Zimbabwe side. This is not meant as a criticism, more as confirmation that he treats every game the same, as an opportunity to score runs and force a win. Sri Lankans may often play an exotic brand of cricket with smiles on their faces, but they are tough competitors with a fervent desire not to be taken for granted.

Sangakkara's innings are tailored to the situations he finds himself in. He does not bat long for the sake of it and one

of his finest hours came against the favourites India in the World Twenty20 final in Dhaka in 2014 when he shook off a run of low scores to guide Sri Lanka to the trophy with an unbeaten half-century in 33 balls. That was a special day for several senior Sri Lankan players who had reached a number of major one-day finals without being able to emulate the 50-overs World Cup triumph of 1996. Modern players are inevitably judged by what they do in one-day cricket as well as Tests and Sangakkara was a focal point of the Sri Lanka one-day side that lost two World Cup finals and two World Twenty20 finals between 2007 and 2012. It was after the loss to India in the 2011 World Cup final that he stepped down as Sri Lanka captain.

Sangakkara puts down his ability to cope on pitches outside the subcontinent to having learnt the game on the Asgiriya school ground in Kandy, which was also used to stage Test matches for many years. The ball bounced and moved around there more than at most Sri Lankan venues, and gave him a head start when he toured places like Australia, New Zealand, South Africa and England. He has scored more than 5,000 Test runs outside his home country at an average of well over 50, a record only a few Asian batsmen can match. Compare his record away from home, for example, to that of Mahela Jayawardene, himself an immense figure in Sri Lankan cricket and Sangakkara's partner-in-crime for many years (they shared numerous big stands together, including a world record partnership of 624 against South Africa in Colombo). Unlike Sangakkara, Jayawardene was never quite as influential overseas as he was at home, averaging less than 40 in Tests outside Sri Lanka.

For a while one of the few blemishes on Sangakkara's CV was the absence of a Test century on English soil but he put that right on his third tour with a fighting hundred to save the match at Southampton in 2011. Three years later, he went better still by playing a lead role in Sri Lanka's first Test series win in England, scoring 147 and 61 at Lord's, where they only just hung on for a draw, and a pair of 50s in their dramatic victory at Headingley.

As many of the finest batsmen seem to, Sangakkara got wiser and even better as the years went by. In 2014, the year in which he turned 37, he scored more international runs than he ever had before and remarkably for the fourth time topped 1,000 runs both in Tests and in one-day internationals. Only one other batsman – Ricky Ponting – had performed this feat even twice. His golden form continued in the first week of 2015 with a double century out of a team score of 356 against a very decent New Zealand pace attack in good bowling conditions in Wellington, after which he said he might review his plan to retire from all international cricket after the World Cup. Why give up when things are going so well?

40. DALE STEYN

South Africa, 2004–

Dale Steyn is the finest fast bowler in the world today. Mitchell Johnson has been as destructive in recent times but Johnson's revival is relatively short-lived and before the winter of 2013–14 his was a mercurial talent. Steyn has been consistently excellent for many years now: fast, accurate and capable of swinging the ball, and utterly focused on his job of spearheading the South Africa attack. Few genuinely fast bowlers seem able to survive the modern merry-go-round

of tours and tournaments; he is one who has, even if he has been spared the occasional one-day commitment. He is a precious commodity and one of the main reasons why South Africa have been so strong.

Short in stature, he is perhaps more like Malcolm Marshall in method than any other fast bowler in our list. At 5ft 10in, he actually stands an inch shorter than Marshall, but the problems he poses are essentially the same. They both moved the ball at high pace, and that is a devilishly hard challenge for any batsman to solve. If there was one secret to their magnificent knack of taking wickets, that was it.

They took their wickets in similar ways, with the stumps and pads threatened on a regular basis but the outside edge also vulnerable to the ball that nipped away late. Perhaps Marshall was slightly more adept at darting the ball back in to the right-hander's pads. Both had exceptionally good records in Asia where fast bowlers generally find the going hard, a reflection that with their lower trajectories they needed less bounce than many of their type to cause problems.

As Steyn will not turn 32 until June 2015, he could yet push Glenn McGrath's record of 563 wickets, the most by any fast bowler in Tests. He is truly a man for all seasons and all conditions. He has won Test matches in every Test-playing country in the world, taking ten wickets in Nagpur, ten in Melbourne, nine in Galle, eight in Trinidad and seven in Karachi. England is the only place where his wickets have cost more than 30 but even there he has helped South Africa win two series and bowled superbly at The Oval in 2012 to take five for 56 in the second innings on a pitch on which South Africa had earlier made 637 for two. He has also been involved in two winning tours of Australia – no easy place to come away with a result – in 2008–09 and 2012–13.

He was only 24 years old when he had what must rank as

one of the greatest seasons any bowler has ever experienced. In fact, statistically, his haul of 78 wickets during the 2007–08 season has never been bettered. What was so impressive about it was that it involved tours of Pakistan, Bangladesh and India, as well as home series against New Zealand and West Indies, and he proved himself to be a threat whatever the opposition, whatever the surface. He had previously played 11 Tests in three years, starting at home against England in 2004–05, and shown promise of great things to come, but this was his big breakthrough.

Like Marshall, Steyn formed a very successful partnership with a beanpole partner who gave the batsmen something very different to think about from the other end – different height, different bounce, different threats to their welfare. Whereas Marshall had Joel Garner for company as his new-ball partner in the mid-1980s, Steyn has worked in tandem with Morne Morkel for the greater part of his international career. Morkel has been less consistent than Garner, who was almost as dangerous as Marshall himself, but when he got things right he and Steyn could be almost unmanageable, as England discovered at the Wanderers in 2010 when they were bowled out twice in less than 50 overs on a pitch with pace and bounce. It is to Steyn's credit that he has carried the attack so well on the occasions when Morkel failed to fire.

Manicured pitches and a general shortage of out-and-out fast bowlers has left the modern batsman quite pampered, but then along came the likes of Steyn and Johnson to shake them out of their complacency. Steyn has done that to even the best players: just as he discomfited England in Johannesburg, so he has caused others unease. On the same ground in 2013, he returned match figures of 11 for 60 against a Pakistan side whose first-innings capitulation for 49 said more about the quality of the bowling from Steyn (who took six for eight), Morkel and Vernon Philander than their lack of appetite for the fight. Steyn's own insatiable hunger for bowling was illustrated by him ending the match with a spell of 11 overs, even though he had already claimed his tenth wicket of the game. The previous month Steyn had played a less prominent part in New Zealand being dismissed for 42 in Cape Town.

Just as batsmen were uneasy at the pace Steyn generated, so he relished the anxiety he caused. He could frighten top-order batsmen as well as tail-enders such as James Anderson, whom he peppered at Headingley in 2008 when Anderson acted as nightwatchman. Asked to describe his role in the lead-up to the 2012 Test series in England, he said, 'I'm just trying to be the fastest bowler South Africa has when we walk out on to the field. That's my job. There's times I can bowl as quickly as anybody in the world … Frankly, I just want to take wickets and scare the s**t out of people.' Jeff Thomson could not have put it more succinctly.

Of the bowlers with more than 350 Test wickets to their name, no one – not even Marshall – has a strike rate to compare with Steyn's figure in the low 40s.

39. AB DE VILLIERS

South Africa 2004–

AB de Villiers is a very modern cricketer – an athletic fielder, an occasional but extremely capable wicketkeeper, a captain, and a very versatile batsman with a reputation firmly established across all formats of the game. He averages more than 50 in both Test cricket and one-day internationals, something only his South Africa teammate Hashim Amla can also claim to have done, and is a star of the Twenty20 format, especially the Indian Premier League. There is perhaps no better finisher in limited-overs cricket today.

Like Kevin Pietersen he has the ability to play ridiculous shots and get away with it, making something very difficult look beguilingly simple. On that basis alone, he stands out as something special. Twenty20 has influenced all types of one-day cricket and made them very different from how they used to be. No target is seemingly beyond reach these days and de Villiers has made a speciality of remaining cool when faced with an improbably stiff run-chase. His talent for winning one-day internationals has blossomed in parallel with the experience he has gained playing in the IPL, to the point where a successful South Africa chase that does not involve de Villiers seeing them across the line has become a rarity.

He seems to know where the ball is going to be bowled almost before the bowler does and by dancing around the crease on lightning quick feet he is able to get himself into position to manufacture the most amazing shots. He scoops deliveries over his left shoulder for six, levers near-yorkers over the extra cover boundary, and plays all manner of shots down the ground. Excelling during his schooldays at a variety of sports such as tennis, rugby, hockey and golf probably helped him hone his phenomenal hand-eye coordination and speed. He runs like the wind between the wickets.

Not that he did much running during a one-day international against West Indies in January 2015 in the helpfully high-altitude conditions of Johannesburg. Persuaded to promote himself to number 3 after South Africa's first wicket fell at 247 in the 39th over, de Villiers

unleashed the fiercest assault ever seen in an international match, racing to 50 off 16 balls and his hundred off 31, thus slicing five balls off the previous record for a century. By the time he was out in the final over, he had plundered 149 off just 44 balls, 16 of which he hit for six. Truly stupendous stuff.

It perhaps says something about the modern game that some of his most extraordinary performances have come in ODIs and Twenty20. England's followers possibly do not need reminding of the innings he played against their side at the World Twenty20 in Chittagong in 2014, in a game England needed to win to stay in the tournament. They weren't doing too badly until de Villiers went into overdrive and the last four overs of the innings saw South Africa's total boosted by 68: after a relatively sedate start he finished with 69 off 28 balls.

In similar but even more spectacular vein were a couple of efforts for Royal Challengers Bangalore in the IPL at the sharp end of run-chases. Both involved him going toe-to-toe with Dale Steyn, so often a friend in South African colours but on these occasions very much the foe, and, as Steyn showed in some of the games at the World Twenty20 in 2014, one of the most difficult bowlers in the world to score off. In 2012, when Steyn was playing for Deccan Chargers, de Villiers faced him for the 18th over of the innings with 39 needed off three overs, surely a tall order for anyone. Not for de Villiers: with some outrageous improvisations, he took 23 off the over, which included a yorker-length ball drilled over extra cover for six. He then took 14 off the first three balls of the next over, so Bangalore actually ended up winning with seven balls to spare.

Two years later, with Steyn now playing for Sunrisers Hyderabad, de Villiers took Bangalore home with an unbeaten 89 off 41 balls, of which 22 came off the penultimate over bowled by Steyn by means of three sixes and a four. Possibly de Villiers knows Steyn's game too well.

What is impressive is that he plays a quite different game for South Africa in Tests, where he generally bats in the middle order at a more measured rate. Whereas someone like Pietersen often seemed to bring his one-day approach into the Test arena, de Villiers takes fewer calculated risks in the five-day game and is usually happy to wait for the bad balls to come along, and then put them away with unerring precision. Mind you, he has been known to step on the gas, as he did at Perth in 2012 when after a careful start he added 98 in a session against a flagging Australia attack. He was briefly the holder of the record score for South Africa with the 278 he made against Pakistan at Abu Dhabi in 2010; two years later Amla displaced him with a triple century against England.

His versatility and adaptability have been greatly to South Africa's advantage. In his early days as a Test player, he kept wicket and opened the batting alongside Graeme Smith, and although he did reasonably well it was a lot to ask, and did not seem to be making best use of his talents. He dropped down the order where his capacity to tailor his game according to the situation stood out. He became the regular keeper in ODIs and then, following Mark Boucher's cruel injury during the tour of England in 2012, took up the gloves again in the Test side for the best part of two years, during which his batting hardly suffered from the imposition. In 2012, he became captain of the 50-overs side and, briefly, the 20-overs side as well.

By the age of 30 de Villiers had 40 international hundreds to his name and it seems that in the years ahead there is not much that he will not be able to do, provided he stays as wonderfully grounded as he has so far. It is hard to imagine that there are not plenty more great days ahead.

38. FRED TRUEMAN

England 1952–65

Fred Trueman was not only a great fast bowler, he was also a great entertainer. There is a theatrical element to bowling fast and Fred played it for all it was worth. He'd happily go into the opposition dressing room before play – in a county match if not a Test match – and announce to the assembled audience which batsmen he'd be getting out later in the day, and how. You can only really play that game if you have the talent to back it up more often than not, and he did. The fact that he played in an era when television, for the first time, was making stars out of top sportsmen may have helped in the nurturing of the image, but if he was the first to talk himself up, soon enough plenty of others were following suit.

The downside to this was that the black-and-white footage of Trueman in action survived for later generations to scrutinise and plenty concluded that he was not quite as fast as the legend – burnished of course by Fred himself – would have them believe. Make no mistake, though, Trueman was fast in his early days and as time went on he developed into a highly skilful operator who did not need pace alone to pick up wickets. In his mature years, he was a highly intelligent operator. He had a lovely action, perfectly honed to the job in hand. You do not become the first bowler in the history of the game to take 300 Test wickets, which Trueman did in 1964, without being very good. His average of 21.57 and strike rate of 49.43 are both exceptional.

The way Trueman burst on to the scene at the age of 21 may have had something to do with how his story unfolded.

England had craved a fast bowler of genuine hostility since the days of Harold Larwood, and when in his first match India lost their first four second-innings wickets for no runs, three of them to Trueman, there was understandable excitement, not least from the bowler himself who sent the Indian batsmen on their way with a few choice words. That, after all, was how a fast bowler was supposed to behave – according to some! Later in the series, Trueman destroyed the Indians in even more comprehensive fashion, taking eight for 31 in a mere 8.4 overs. 'Where would you like the sightscreen, batsman?' 'Between myself and Mr Trueman, thank you.'

The aura was established but it took Trueman time to adjust to the reputation he had won. On his first England tour to the Caribbean in 1953–54 his immaturity got the better of him as he showed little concern at the manner in which he injured some of the West Indies batsmen, one of whom was the greatly respected George Headley. He lost his good conduct bonus and played only three Tests in the next three years.

The penny dropped in the end and from the time that he got his England place back for an extended run in 1957 he embarked on a golden period in his career, and the one predicted for him when he first emerged from the South Yorkshire mining community to excite the coaches at Headingley. He took 22 wickets at just over 20 apiece in that summer's series with West Indies, which England won 3–0, and he took 15 more at 17.06 against New Zealand the following year. The realisation dawned that a new-ball pairing of Trueman and Brian Statham could be a winning combination. Between May 1957 and May 1963, Trueman took 197 Test wickets and Statham 132, Trueman at the much superior average and strike rate.

Although he had some natural gifts such as strength and speed, by Trueman's own admission it took him several years to fully master his craft. He learnt to pitch the ball up to allow it to swing late. He commanded a big out-swinger but also a deadly off-cutter, as well as a very good yorker. Although he became a very canny analyst of conditions as well as the strengths and weaknesses of opponents, there was still the occasional disaster where he lost the plot, as happened at Headingley in 1964 when he tried and spectacularly failed to bounce out Australia's Peter Burge. It cost England the game. But against the same opponents on the same ground three years earlier he had bowled brilliantly in victory.

For four years from 1959, Trueman was outstanding, taking 20 or more wickets in seven out of eight successive series. Although his overall record in England was exceptional he was also very good on tours of the West Indies and Australia. England won in the Caribbean in 1959–60, which was a terrific achievement given that the West Indies batting included the likes of Garry Sobers and Frank Worrell, and came away with a draw – if not the Ashes – in Australia in 1962–63. The one game that England won in each series owed much to Trueman, who took five for 35 in the first innings in Trinidad and eight wickets in the game at Melbourne.

If Trueman's home and away records are lopsided it is partly because he was selected for so few overseas tours in his early days. That said, his figures in England accurately reflected how dangerous he was when the ball moved around: he took 229 wickets at home at a shade over 20 each and a strike rate of 44.9. Jim Laker and Tony Lock took their Test wickets in England more cheaply but none of England's leading bowlers can improve on Trueman's strike rate in home matches. Not until James Anderson overtook him in 2014 did anyone beat his haul of wickets in England.

In retirement, Fred almost became a caricature of himself, whether as a radio summariser or as a regular voice on the after-dinner circuit. He was disappointed at some of the things that might have been – he would have liked the Yorkshire captaincy but it never came his way – and decried what he saw as declining standards. In truth he was never quite the character of popular myth. He was not a big drinker, nor really a fire-breathing monster. But it had served to think he was. As John Warr, another England bowler, once said of Trueman, 'Cricket and the Anglo-Saxon tongue have been enriched by his presence.'

37. GREG CHAPPELL

Australia 1970–84

When Greg Chappell retired from Test cricket in 1984, it was widely accepted that he was the best batsman Australia had produced since Don Bradman. His Test record certainly suggested as much: by scoring 182 against Pakistan in his final Test innings, he overtook Bradman's run tally in Tests and finished with a career average of 53.86 that was second only to Bradman's among Australians. On top of that, though, should be taken into account what he did in Kerry Packer's World Series, which was every bit as good as the 'Establishment' cricket of the period. In 14 World Series 'Supertests' he scored 1,415 runs at an average of 56.60, which was the best overall record of any batsman – more runs at a slightly better average than Viv Richards, who had the considerable advantage of not having to deal with the

West Indies pace battery. New Zealand's Richard Hadlee said Chappell was the best batsman he bowled to.

Along with his elder brother Ian, who captained the side before him, Dennis Lillee and Jeff Thomson, Greg was one of the main reasons why Australia were the best team in the world before West Indies rose to the top in the late 1970s. Ian was a mighty fine batsman in his own right, though very different in style. Whereas Ian was the rugged Chappell, Greg was the more beautiful version. Greg was technically better – and better to watch. I first got to know him relatively late in his career, when World Series had finished and both England and West Indies toured Australia at the same time. It was a move designed, I suppose, to showcase the best of official Test cricket once all the star performers were back in the fold, but England did not really approve and refused to put the Ashes urn up for grabs (a shrewd decision: Australia thrashed us in all three Tests). For me, as a 22-year-old, to mingle with the top Australian guys, having previously toured and faced their second XI, was a great thrill. There was an aura about them. Greg scored a fine hundred in the final match of that series and made two more when we returned, this time with the Ashes at stake, three winters later in 1982–83.

I always found Greg reasonable and got to know him pretty well. He was actually a big help to me when I went through my first slump in Test cricket. The Australians were in England towards the end of the 1980 season for the Centenary Test and through the kind auspices of Fred Rumsey, who was a surrogate father to me and knew Greg from Greg's time at Somerset early in his career, a meeting was arranged between the two of us. Fred thought Greg might be able to impart some useful advice about playing Test cricket and he was right. Greg was interesting and sympathetic. What was clear was that he knew a lot about his subject. He said for instance that when he first went in he would consciously seek to play with the inside half of the bat to cover for any away movement. It wasn't something I sought to copy – I dared not complicate things any more than they were already – but it showed me the level of detail into which some of the best players went. Much later, I worked alongside him in the commentary box for Channel Nine, and I formed the same impression of a very talented, analytical and competitive person (this was a man, remember, who once controversially instructed his other brother Trevor to bowl underarm in a one-dayer to deny New Zealand victory).

Greg may, in fact, have been a little too analytical for his own good. As time went on, he certainly seemed to find the responsibility of being Australia's captain and leading batsman a strain (he led them in 48 of his 87 Test matches). He took the unusual step for a serving captain of missing a couple of big series, including the 1981 tour of England, which might well not have gone so badly for Australia had he opted to lead the side rather than hand the reins to Kim Hughes. Having done so well against the very best of the West Indian fast bowlers, the barrage finally seemed to catch up with him during the 1981–82 season when Australia hosted tours by West Indies and Pakistan, who themselves had fine fast bowlers in Imran Khan and Sarfraz Nawaz. For a period his form collapsed and he fell for seven ducks in the space of 15 international innings, a bad run by anyone's standards. He was so concerned he even took himself off to have his eyes tested. Fortunately the crisis proved short-lived.

Interestingly, too, Greg's time as coach of India ended unhappily, with even Sachin Tendulkar, who does not lightly offer criticism, saying that Greg had not been popular with the players and had failed to take the team forward.

Greg learnt a lot from his two seasons at Somerset in the late 1960s and by the time he was brought into the Australia side during the 1970–71 Ashes series was more than ready to take the step up to the international arena. Tall, slim and always well balanced in his movements, he displayed a masterly technique but also the soundest of temperaments as he stroked an effortless century in his first innings that belied the difficult situation his team was in when he reached the crease. From the very start, he clearly belonged in the biggest arena. He came to England in 1972, and scored hundreds at both Lord's and The Oval in the two games Australia won. In Wellington in 1974, he scored 247 in the first innings and 133 in the second for a match aggregate of 380 that was not beaten until Graham Gooch (333 and 123 against India) went past him in 1990.

Greg was also one of the finest slip fielders the game has seen. He retired with 122 catches to his name, seven of them in one game against England at Perth. The former was then a Test record; the latter still is.

36. HERBERT SUTCLIFFE

England 1924–35

Herbert Sutcliffe was one of England's toughest cricketers. He said he wasn't as good as Jack Hobbs, with whom he formed a famous Test match opening partnership, Wally Hammond or Len Hutton, but he had amazing powers of concentration and tenacity, and averaged more in Tests than any of them, and indeed more in Ashes Tests than anyone bar Don Bradman. Bradman's opinion was that Sutcliffe had the best temperament of any cricketer he played with or against. The hundred he scored in the fourth innings on a rain-affected wicket at Melbourne in 1929 to take England to within sight of the finishing line in what remains their highest successful run-chase, must rank among the greatest ever scored.

That performance typified Sutcliffe. He did not mind how uncomfortable he might look, or how many blows he might take to the body (and on that occasion balls were kicking up around his head), as long as he survived. He was courageous, unflappable, and expert at leaving balls that did not need to be played – all good qualities in an opener, and qualities that earned him his place in the distinguished line of outstanding Yorkshire and England openers that also included Len Hutton and Geoffrey Boycott. Sutcliffe played a big role in mentoring Hutton, who like Sutcliffe played his early cricket around Pudsey.

He was as reliable a Test match opener as there has been. He was only dismissed without scoring twice and no regular opener for any country has ever averaged more than Sutcliffe's 61.10 going in first for England; in Hobbs he found the ideal partner. Their productivity in what in modern terms was quite a short period was remarkable: in 39 opening stands between 1924 and 1930, when Hobbs retired from Test cricket, they scored 3,339 runs together, included in which were 15 century partnerships. Perhaps their most famous stand together came in the final Test in 1926 with the Ashes at stake when they both scored masterly centuries on another pitch made difficult by rain. England eventually ran out decisive winners. Despite the proliferation of Test cricket since, only one opening pair – the West Indians Desmond Haynes and Gordon Greenidge

– have posted more three-figure starts. Sutcliffe also formed another special relationship with Percy Holmes at Yorkshire; they shared 69 century stands for the first wicket, including what for many years was a world record 555 against Essex at Leyton in 1932.

Sutcliffe's technique was not flawless. He was reckoned to play with an open face and spinners thought they could have him caught close in on the off side. Bill O'Reilly and Clarrie Grimmett had some success against him but he still averaged at least 50 in every series he played against Australia. He was not afraid to hook fast bowling – no helmets in those days, remember – and although he tended to hit the ball in the air when he did so, it was a shot that served him well. It was about the only risk he indulged in. He was generally a superb player of the fastest bowling.

At his peak between the years of 1927 to 1933, in six English seasons and two tours of Australia and one of South Africa, Sutcliffe scored almost 20,000 runs at an average of 66.72. These were days of good batting pitches and high scoring, but even so Sutcliffe stood out among his English peers. He relished the biggest challenges and Test matches against Australia, and Yorkshire's battles with Lancashire, which were then great occasions, almost always saw him at his best. Yorkshire and Lancashire were the dominant counties of the period, Yorkshire winning 12 championships and Lancashire five in the 21 seasons between 1919 and 1939 that formed Sutcliffe's career.

The First World War delayed his entry into county cricket until he was 24 years old but he had played some cricket during the war while serving in the military and made an immediate impact with Yorkshire's first team, scoring what remains a record 1,839 runs for someone in their debut season. Although his next two seasons proved quite fallow he began to tighten up his game and in 1922 topped 2,000 for the first of what turned out to be 14 straight seasons.

He was in his 30th year when he made his Test debut against South Africa in 1924, scoring 64 in his first match, 122 in his second and 83 and 29 not out in his third. The following winter he made his first tour and found Australian pitches, and the format of Test matches played to a finish, to his liking. Australia won the series 4–1 but Sutcliffe was unperturbed, occupying the crease for more than 30 hours and 712 runs in the first four matches before exhaustion appeared to take its toll in the final contest. He scored 59 and 115 in the opening Test in Sydney, which lasted seven days, before moving on to Melbourne for the second game, which started five days later and itself lasted seven days. There he batted 13½ hours, scoring 176 in the first innings – batting right through the third day in a stand of 283 with Hobbs – and 127 in the second.

In all first-class cricket, Sutcliffe scored 50,135 runs (placing him seventh on the all-time list) and 149 centuries (which puts him sixth), and his Test average of 60.73 is the highest among all Englishmen, with only Bradman (99.94), Graeme Pollock (60.97) and George Headley (60.83) standing ahead of him. His stature went beyond mere figures though. He took immense pride in his appearance, and was always immaculately turned out, and was offered – but declined – the position of Yorkshire's first modern professional captain. In retirement he became a successful businessman, developing a sports outfitting company.

35. FRANK WORRELL

West Indies 1948–63

If cricket in the West Indies was ever united, it was thanks to Frank Worrell's captaincy. He actually only led the Test team in three series, taking in tours of Australia and England, and a visit to the Caribbean by India, but his appointment in 1960 was the culmination of a long campaign on the part of others to see a black man officially appointed captain of the West Indies team, and of Worrell's own work in the cause of social equality. Having been born and raised in Barbados before relocating to Trinidad and Jamaica, he had little time for inter-island rivalry and pettiness.

Partly through his own considerable ability as an all-round player, as well as his charismatic leadership, Worrell left West Indies the strongest team in the world and created something of a blueprint for Clive Lloyd when he returned West Indies to the summit of the game some 15 years later. It says something about Worrell that although his team lost in Australia in 1960–61, he and his players were fêted through the streets of Melbourne when they left, and in time when Australia and West Indies met they competed for the Frank Worrell Trophy. Worrell's side were also saluted for their style and class in England in 1963 (when they won 3–1) and he was given a knighthood the following year. A distinguished career in politics might have followed – he was appointed senator in the Jamaica parliament – but tragically he died of leukaemia at the age of just 42.

Given the pressure he was under to prove himself, especially as West Indies had suffered a string of defeats to

England and Australia in the years beforehand, Worrell did not seek popularity when the captaincy came to him at the age of 35, but that was certainly what he achieved.

As a batsman, he was both courageous and cultured, certainly the most technically correct and stylish of the 'three Ws' even if his figures were not as impressive as those of Everton Weekes or Clyde Walcott. He scored 3,860 runs at an average of 49.48 in his 51 Test matches with nine hundreds but he missed some good years when he might have scored heavily, appearing in only one Test series between 1955 and 1960, in part because he took an economics degree at Manchester University. In the one series he did play during that period, in England in 1957, he turned his hand to opening at Trent Bridge and carried his bat for 191, an effort that went a long way towards saving the game. In the following match at Headingley he showed his talent as a left-arm swing bowler by taking seven for 70 (he took 69 Test wickets in all). Playing his first Test for three years at Barbados in 1960, he batted through two days with Garry Sobers, and for almost 11½ hours in all, for 197 against Peter May's England side.

His batting probably suffered from the demands of leadership. Although he averaged 40 as captain, and played some important innings, he did not convert any of his ten 50s into hundreds.

Worrell was first chosen for Barbados for his spin bowling; it was during the war and he was just 17 years old. It was not long before his batting talent manifested itself though, and in spectacular fashion. He was still only 19 when he scored an unbeaten triple century against Trinidad, in the process sharing in a stand of 502 with John Goddard. Two years later he and Walcott gave Trinidad's bowlers further punishment, putting on a then world record 574 together, Worrell's share being 255.

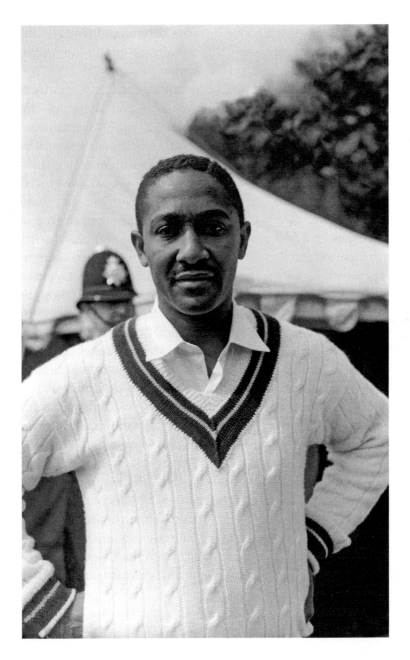

He dismissed both feats as unimportant but they reflected his potential, a potential that was swiftly realised when he played his first Test matches against a touring England side in 1948 (it was not a full-strength England attack but contained a young Jim Laker). Worrell scored 97 in his first game and an unbeaten 131 in his second. He then joined Radcliffe in the Central Lancashire League, a move that he said transformed his game. He scored heavily as a member of a Commonwealth XI that toured India, Pakistan and Ceylon (as it then was) in 1949–50 and 1950–51, and as occasional captain he learnt something about bringing together men of different backgrounds.

If his last tours of Australia and England showed the best of Worrell as leader, his first tours of those places saw him at his best as a player. The West Indian team of 1950 that won in England for the first time was one of the most glamorous of all visiting sides: Weekes, Worrell and Walcott and those little pals Sonny Ramadhin and Alf Valentine. England's landslide victory in the first Test – Worrell stumped twice batting at number 3 – proved a mirage. West Indies steamrollered them in three subsequent matches and Worrell was to the fore with 261 at Trent Bridge (the highest Test innings for a West Indian in England until Viv Richards's 291 in 1976) and 138 at The Oval.

That series prompted the hope that West Indies might also push Australia hard at home in 1951–52 but they were unable to withstand the overt hostility of Ray Lindwall and Keith Miller. There was however no cowing Worrell, who batted bravely and unflappably for 108 and 30 at Melbourne after a blow from Miller left him batting virtually one-handed. It was not quite enough to prevent Australia winning by one wicket. Worrell's bowling was a major factor in the one match West Indies did win in Adelaide, where on a damp pitch he took six for 38 bowling unchanged as Australia were dismissed for 82.

Worrell's death was marked by a memorial service in Westminster Abbey, the only cricketer to be accorded such treatment. Learie Constantine described him as 'a happy man, a good man and a great man'.

34. RICKY PONTING

Australia 1995–2012

Ricky Ponting was the best batsman produced by Australia since Don Bradman and a highly capable leader of their side. He led them to two World Cup wins but will also be remembered as the first Australia captain in almost 20 years to lose a Test series to England. It was an experience he ended up enduring three times, but after the defeat in 2005 he could not have supervised a more emphatic response than the 16 Test wins his side then produced off the reel, including a 5–0 whitewash of England in which he personally weighed in with 576 runs. He was unlucky that his final years coincided with the decline of a once-great side but he always conducted himself with dignity, even when English crowds took to treating him as a pantomime villain on the 2009 tour. He was utterly selfless.

He was hardly the conventional choice to succeed Steve Waugh, first in one-dayers in 2002 and then in Tests two years later, but it proved an inspired decision. Growing up in public as a precociously talented youngster is not easy and Ponting, the wild boy from Tasmania who was only

two months past his 20th birthday when first capped by his country, needed to learn some early lessons along the way. There was a well-publicised incident in a Sydney nightclub which left him with a black eye. But his response was impressive. He apologised to his teammates for letting them down and focused on channelling his competitiveness in the right direction. The respect of your teammates is a vital thing in cricket and Ponting earned it with his willingness to change and improve, as well as his sheer class as a player. Good judges in Australia were predicting great things for him at a very early stage.

As a batsman, Ponting in full flow was a beautiful sight. He was always very positive and quick on to the ball. His attitude was that the ball was there to be hit: his instinct was to look to score before he thought of defence. The swivel-pull off the front foot was a trademark shot of his, as was the straight drive down the ground to balls full on off stump. He was as adept at one-day cricket as he was in Tests. He scored more than 13,000 runs in both formats, putting him, at the time of his retirement, second on both lists behind Sachin Tendulkar (also the only player with more international hundreds than Ponting's 71).

In many ways, he was almost ridiculously eager to get on to the front foot, certainly for an Australian, and therefore I suspect the helmet was a vital part of his equipment. That certainly does not mean that he was in any way short of courage and he didn't shrink from taking on the fast men, even when Steve Harmison gashed his cheek at Lord's in 2005. Three games later he played one of the finest – if not the finest – innings of his career by batting throughout most of the final day for 156 to save the Test at Old Trafford against Harmison and Andrew Flintoff when they were near their peaks.

If he had a flaw it was that because he was coming forward all the time he was vulnerable early in his innings to balls just outside off stump, and if he was not moving well then to straight deliveries as well. This was probably why he averaged in the low 40s in Tests in England where the new ball can nibble around. In Australia, where the new ball does less, and for a shorter time, his record was immense – more runs (7,578) and centuries (23) than anyone else has ever managed, at an average of 56.97. Once he was in, there was very little shifting him. He had problems too with Indian spinners Harbhajan Singh and Anil Kumble in their own conditions, in which he scored only one hundred, but he is not alone in discovering that Asian spinners in Asian conditions are harder to combat.

Ponting naturally led from the front. He started out in the lower middle order but he found his niche at first wicket down, a position he held – amazingly, given the sheer volume of cricket involved – for ten years from the England tour of 2001 until he dropped a place or two after Michael Clarke took over the captaincy from him in 2011. For all that time, he was the rock on which the Australian batting was built. Number 3 is a position that demands great versatility, sometimes playing like an opener when an early wicket falls, at other times driving home an advantage if the first-wicket pair have given the side a good start, which of course Matthew Hayden and Justin Langer often did.

The captaincy could hardly be said to have had a detrimental effect on his batting, which is to his immense credit as he held the Test job for almost seven years and the one-day post for ten. He averaged 52.18 in Tests when he was not in charge and 51.51 when he was. If Old Trafford 2005 saw the best of him in defensive mode, Adelaide 2006 was him at his attacking best. There he delivered a stirring speech to his men on the third morning of the game to the effect that the match could still be won despite England scoring 551 in their first innings. He proceeded to score a hundred, Australia got close enough to England's score to put the pressure back on them, and Australia duly pulled off a miracle win. In the World Cup final of 2003 in Johannesburg, his unbeaten 140 off 121 balls provided a masterclass in how to accelerate through a one-day innings, and put the game beyond India's reach.

Perhaps his positive thinking occasionally got the better of him, such as the time he put England in to bat on a good pitch at Edgbaston in 2005, a decision that arguably marked the turning point of the series and has been roundly derided since by Shane Warne, but generally his approach fitted Australia's ultra-attacking style of play and brought about far more good than bad. He was also an outstanding fielder: a fine catcher, and a brilliant interceptor in the covers or at midwicket, from where he brought about many run-outs.

33. JAVED MIANDAD

Pakistan 1976–93

Like many great Asian batsmen, Javed Miandad was immense on his own pitches, but in his case he was also versatile and skilful enough to make Test hundreds when the ball was behaving very differently in Australia, England and the Caribbean. Spotted at an early age by Mushtaq Mohammad as a great player in the making, he seemed to be born with a good technique. He scored a century in his first Test match and a double century in his third. He was still in his early twenties when he scored centuries against Richard Hadlee in Christchurch and Rodney Hogg at the WACA, and more than 2,000 runs in a championship season for Glamorgan. He was the star batsman at the World Cup that Pakistan won in Australia and New Zealand in 1992, making runs in every match but one, including half-centuries in the semi-final and final, when his partnership of 139 with Imran Khan laid the platform for victory over England. Imran had asked his players to fight like cornered tigers at that tournament, and no one fought harder than Javed.

If the art of batting is allied to the ability to watch the ball closely, then Javed was an absolute master. I've seen him play balls right in front of his face when the instinct of most people would be to duck their head behind their hands. There was none of that with him. He watched the ball right on to the bat and knocked it down, a model of control. He was brave and courageous. There was no fear.

His unorthodox game was in fact ideally suited to one-day cricket, a format that was just developing into a global product when he arrived on the scene in the mid-1970s (he actually played in each of the first six World Cups between 1975 and 1996, a testament to his talent and durability). He had quick feet and supple wrists, and a great facility for manoeuvring the ball into the gaps, a vital skill in the middle overs of a one-day innings. He was a master at letting the ball come to him, playing it late and using its pace to his advantage with neat deflections into the gaps. He cottoned on at an early stage that it was not always necessary to bludgeon the ball. He must rank as one of the best and earliest 'finishers' in one-day cricket.

His one-day record does not look particularly striking to today's eyes but when he retired in 1996 only Desmond

Haynes had scored more runs in ODIs and few could better his average of 41.70. What is especially notable, though, is how he performed in matches Pakistan won when chasing: he finished unbeaten in almost half his innings and averaged 66.24. His most famous feat in this regard, and one for which he is as well remembered in Pakistan as for anything else he did, was hitting a six off the last ball of the match, when four were needed, from Chetan Sharma to win an Asia Cup final in Sharjah.

He may have been a shot-maker by instinct but he could play the longer game, as his Test match résumé clearly shows. His 8,832 runs at an average of 52.57 from 124 matches remains the most for Pakistan – Inzamam-ul-Haq failed to match him by only two runs – and it should be remembered that runs were not so easy to come by in the 1980s as they were later when pitches and pace attacks became more docile. There were only four individual Test scores of more than 250 during that decade and Javed made three of them. His ten-hour 260 at The Oval in 1987 firmly killed off our chances of levelling the series.

His record against West Indies, the powerhouse of that period, was understandably mixed, but he played a big part in an epic series in the Caribbean in 1988 in which Pakistan became the first visiting side to hold their own, earning a 1–1 draw. Javed scored a battling hundred in the match Pakistan won in Guyana and another in the fourth innings in Trinidad as his team successfully held out for a draw by batting out 129 overs (they actually needed only 31 more for victory when the match ended with them nine down).

His unpredictability was probably one of his greatest strengths. Ray Illingworth, my first captain at Leicestershire, used to like to give himself an exploratory over just before lunch, just to see if the pitch was taking turn, and confident in the knowledge that batsmen were unlikely to take risks at such a juncture. On one occasion against Sussex, however, he got a rude shock when Javed, who had a spell with them in the late 1970s, saw this merely as an opportunity and promptly whacked him back over his head three times. Illy did not bowl again in the innings.

This would have incensed Illy, and not just because it ruined his lunch, but then needling opponents – and sometimes even teammates – was Javed's speciality. I never had any gripe with him but I know plenty of people who did, including most famously Dennis Lillee, with whom he once very nearly exchanged blows in a Test match at the WACA. He also played a part, as Pakistan captain, in stirring the pot after Mike Gatting's spectacular falling-out with umpire Shakoor Rana at Faisalabad in 1987 which led to the loss of a day's play. He was also captaining Pakistan on the 1992 tour of England on which allegations of ball-tampering left the teams at loggerheads. If trouble was in the air, he could generally be counted on to get involved and I'm sure it was a deliberate ploy. He was a big competitor with a combative spirit, who likened cricket to war.

But Javed also deserves to be remembered as one of Pakistan's best captains. He often stood in when Imran was not available and despite therefore being without the team's best all-rounder had a good record, leading Pakistan to as many Test wins as Imran himself. If Imran was the principal architect behind Pakistan's rise in the 1980s, Javed was not far behind.

32. CURTLY AMBROSE

West Indies, 1988–2000

Curtly Ambrose was a man of few words but many great deeds. He was very similar to Joel Garner in terms of angles and height – he was 6ft 7in to Garner's 6ft 8in, but let's not quibble – but he was perhaps even more relentlessly accurate while also capable of serious speed.

Ambrose led the West Indies attack more often than Garner and for much of his career carried the bowling along with Courtney Walsh, with whom he shared the new ball from 1994 to 2000. He arrived on the scene shortly after Garner and Michael Holding played their final Tests and within three years Malcolm Marshall was also finished. The preferred option remained four fast men but the support acts to Ambrose and Walsh were not of the old calibre. Those two did their bit, though, to continue the grand tradition of menacing Caribbean quicks.

Ambrose was perhaps the most consistently accurate of all genuinely fast bowlers. Of those with 200 Test wickets, only Marshall and Garner had lower averages than Ambrose's 20.99 and in both cases by only a fraction, and Ambrose (98 matches, 405 wickets) played more Tests than either of them. His economy rate of 2.30 is unrivalled by any genuine quick man: the seven with 200 wickets with better economy rates are all from earlier eras: six were primarily spinners while Alec Bedser was a medium-pacer. The key was perhaps that he had an utterly dependable action. He was rarely injured.

Given the workload for those in his position, melding international demands with county and island careers, it is no wonder that at times he saved himself and bowled within himself. It was as if there were two Ambroses. On a quiet day, of which there were not many, he could operate at 70 per cent and still be effective. On a good day, he was far more purposeful, and you could tell that from the way his legs were operating. The higher the knees lifted, the more interested he was. Allan Lamb, a Northamptonshire colleague of his, would say when we were playing against West Indies, 'Hey, Amby's got his knees up today! He's steaming in!' One such time I remember vividly was actually not in a Test but a NatWest Trophy semi-final for Hampshire against Northants at Southampton, with Lamb and Ambrose in the opposition. I got 80-odd but we ended up losing by one run. There was a key period in our chase where Lamb as captain brought back Ambrose, and it was just a matter of keeping him out. The knees were certainly high that day as he made the ball fly past at chest height. He only took one wicket in 12 overs but went for just 29 runs and in the end that was probably the difference.

Knees pumping, he produced some of the greatest spells of fast bowling seen in Test cricket in modern times and could run through a side almost on his own as he homed in on a full length on off stump, fist pumping in celebration at every wicket. I was thankfully watching from the stands when he ripped through England after tea on the final day in Bridgetown in 1990 after it had looked as though Lamb, Robin Smith and Jack Russell, in his finest rearguard mode, would hold out for a draw. I happened to be in Barbados on a pre-season tour with Hampshire and there was some discussion about me joining the reinforcements after injuries had taken their toll but in the end it was decided – rightly and probably thankfully! – that I was short of the match practice. Ambrose's figures that day were a highly impressive eight

for 45, but those paled beside his seven for 25 – including a spell of seven for one in 32 balls – three years later when he blew away Australia at the WACA. He was also the destroyer at Trinidad in 1994 when Michael Atherton's England side were scuttled for 46, an amazing performance given that England had had victory in their sights not long before.

Given the bounce he could generate, it was natural Ambrose should do well in Australia, as he did. He took 26 wickets in the series there in 1988–89 and 33 when West Indies next visited in 1992–93. But he was also skilful enough to make the most of English conditions, in which he wobbled the ball around just enough to be dangerous. He was very new to Test cricket when he came to England in 1988, which was the only series in which I came up against him, and he took 22 wickets at just 20.22. As with Garner, England found him very difficult to keep out, let alone score off. In the seven series he played against England his worst figures by a distance were the 21 wickets he took in the 1995 series in England at a cost of 24.09. His average was either around the 20 mark or in the teens. Overall, he took 164 wickets against England at 18.79 each and 128 against Australia at 21.23.

These were the big series in which he routinely did well but he also snatched a win in a Test match against South Africa at Bridgetown in 1992 – South Africa's first after the anti-apartheid boycott was lifted – rather as he did in the England game in Trinidad, when again it looked as though West Indies would lose until Ambrose, in this instance with Walsh's help, made a dramatic late intervention. South Africa were at one stage 123 for two chasing 201, but lost their last eight for 25. No game was ever lost with Ambrose in your side.

The only reservation that could be put against his record is that he played only six Tests in Asia – and none in India

– so it is hard to judge quite how effective he really was on those types of wicket.

31. GEORGE HEADLEY

West Indies 1930–54

George Headley was the first great West Indian batsman and a pioneer for cricket in the Caribbean. Alongside all-rounder Learie Constantine, who was several years older but played with him in many of his Test matches, he did a great deal to put West Indies cricket on the map and accelerate the process of black players being treated more fairly. Headley himself probably ought to have captained West Indies more than the one time – which he did against England in his native Jamaica in 1948 – but at least he broke the tradition of the team being led only by whites. It was a start.

Headley's figures were astonishing, especially for someone batting number 3 in a side without another frontline batsman of real substance, and understandably earned him the sobriquet from Englishmen and Australians of the 'black Bradman' (his supporters preferred to describe Bradman as the 'white Headley') – but there was more to it than that. He made runs when they mattered and enabled West Indies to record some important early victories against the most powerful nations. He himself was not powerfully built. His success was down to a determination to dominate, the quickness of his feet and the precision of his strokes: he was an expert at hitting the gaps in the field, especially on the leg side (Clarrie Grimmett said he never bowled to a stronger leg-side player). He watched the ball like a hawk and played it at the last moment.

He did more than anyone in the 1930s to show that they could compete with the best and that must have been an inspiration to the great West Indies players who came along later such as Garry Sobers, the three Ws, and Sonny Ramadhin and Alf Valentine. Even when I toured the West Indies in 1981, and he came to one of the Tests, his name evoked reverence and admiration among locals.

When West Indies won their first Test match outside the Caribbean, on a rain-affected pitch at Sydney in 1931 that demanded some brave tactics from them, Headley scored a quick century. Then, when they won their first series at home to England in 1934–35, it was Headley's runs that did as much as anything to turn things around after they had lost the first Test. He hit 93, the best individual score of the game, in the victory in Trinidad and an unbeaten 270 that constituted more than half the West Indies total to set up an innings victory in the fourth and final Test on his home island of Jamaica. That stood as the highest score for a West Indian until it was beaten by Sobers's world record (at the time) of 365.

Headley might so easily not have been a cricketer. He was born in Panama where his father, a Bajan, worked on the building of the canal; he spoke Spanish as a child and did not move to Jamaica until he was ten years old. There he lived with relatives and the plan was for him to move to the United States and become a dentist. However, while at school he discovered cricket and dentistry's loss became cricket's gain, although it was a close-run thing. A delay in getting his passport enabled him to play some matches for Jamaica against a touring English side captained by Lionel Tennyson in 1928 and in three games he scored more than

400 runs, including a double century at Melbourne Park in Kingston. He was only 18 years of age. The plan to emigrate was abandoned.

Despite his youth, he probably should have been chosen for West Indies' first full tour of England a few months later, on which they lost all three Tests by big margins, but the selectors did not make the same mistake again.

When an English side next toured West Indies and played four Tests, Headley made an immediate and spectacular impact. The bowling was not the best England had but nor was it the worst (it included a 52-year-old but still canny Wilfred Rhodes as well as Bill Voce). Headley scored 176 in the first Test, 114 and 112 in the third and 223 to save the fourth and thereby ensure the series was drawn 1–1 and England thought carefully in future about the bowlers they put out against the West Indians. The message was reinforced when Tennyson took another side to Jamaica in 1932 and Headley scored 344 not out, 84 and 155 not out, and 140.

Once chosen, Headley appeared in every Test West Indies played up to the Second World War – even though inter-island rivalries meant selection often varied wildly from one home venue to another – and he did not have one bad series, whether in the West Indies, England or Australia. Test matches were of course far less frequent in those days and opportunities for newer international sides such as West Indies were fewer still but there was no arguing with Headley's statistics: in 19 Test matches against England in this period he scored 2,135 runs at an average of 66.71 including ten centuries, two of them doubles. He played a few further games after the war with little success. His overall Test record (2,190 runs, average 60.83) and first-class record (9,921 runs, average 69.86) make him the only person besides Bradman to average more than 60 in both spheres.

There would have been the usual doubts expressed about Headley's ability to translate his big scores in the West Indies to English conditions but when he finally made his first tour of England in 1933 he lived up to expectations, scoring almost twice as many runs as anyone else on his side even though he missed games. His unbeaten 169 earned West Indies a draw in the Old Trafford Test and helped secure him a contract in the Lancashire League with Haslingden, with whom he spent several seasons. When he toured a second time in 1939, he became the first man to score a century in both innings of a Test at Lord's.

30. MUTTIAH MURALITHARAN

Sri Lanka 1992–2010

Perhaps no country has challenged cricket's orthodoxies more than Sri Lanka. In its relatively short life as a Test match nation it has given the game some of its most exotic and original sights: Lasith Malinga's slingy thunderbolts, Sanath Jayasuriya's explosive hitting and Muttiah Muralitharan's extraordinary style of spin. Murali was the first to make an impact and not only traditionalists were baffled by what he did. Batsmen who faced him found that the normal clues as to whether he was bowling a leg-break or an off-break weren't there. No one had ever bowled quite like him before and it was bound to take people time to fathom what he was up to and work out a method (most, of course, never really did). It is not surprising people were suspicious.

It took a while for the controversy to subside sufficiently for all the facts to emerge. The decision of Australia's umpires to call him for throwing during Sri Lanka's tour there in 1995–96 – when he was 23 years old and not yet the seasoned match-winner he later became – generated more heat than light, but gradually the message got home that Murali's bowling arm had possessed a deformity since birth and could never be fully straightened. As testing methods became more thorough, it also transpired that almost all bowlers delivered the ball with a slightly bent arm: a tolerance level of 15 degrees was eventually set which effectively (and some critics said conveniently) allowed Murali to bowl without being called again.

It was a debate that was never going to be resolved to everyone's satisfaction. What also had to be borne in mind was that regardless of what his arm was doing, his wrist had a phenomenal flex of its own; to what extent this depended on movement lower down the arm was merely something else for observers and law-makers to ponder over.

What is beyond argument is that he provided a great spectacle. My abiding image of him is of that look of a wild-eyed, smiling assassin. I loved watching him bowl because he so obviously loved it and wanted to bowl and bowl and bowl (he averaged 55 overs per Test, more than any other leading bowler). When you heard him talk, you could sense how enthusiastic he was about his art. He was a tireless and joyous performer who did not really ever want to give up. He played for Sri Lanka until almost his 40th year and in 2014 at the age of 42 was still turning out in the Indian Premier League, Twenty20 being another format in which he was highly effective. He rarely got slogged.

His figures are unmatched and in all probability uncatchable: his 800 wickets in Test matches and 534 in one-day internationals are both records, as are his number of five-wicket hauls in a Test innings (67, almost double the 37 of his nearest rival Shane Warne) and ten-wicket hauls in a match (22, compared to Warne's ten).

A few months after his traumatic experience in Australia, Murali played an important role in Sri Lanka's World Cup triumph, an event that formally sealed their arrival as a global force. He only took seven wickets in the tournament but in six matches never conceded more than 42 runs in his ten overs (in the final against Australia his figures were 10-0-31-1). Two years later he single-handedly destroyed England in a Test at The Oval with match figures of 16 for 220 (the fifth-best of all time); it was Sri Lanka's first Test win on English soil and another marker in their rise. Murali in partnership with Chaminda Vaas, a very fine left-arm swing bowler who himself claimed 355 Test wickets, gave Sri Lanka the means of winning matches on a regular basis, especially at home.

He did have to reinvent himself in mid-career, though. He had always been slightly less effective against left-handers and as time went on the best of them found ways to counter him to a significant extent. In 2001, England went to Sri Lanka and won thanks in large part to the runs scored by the left-handed Marcus Trescothick and Graham Thorpe. The following year, England won again at home, with Trescothick, Thorpe and Mark Butcher, another left-hander, all scoring hundreds. Although Sri Lanka beat the visiting West Indians 3–0 in 2001 Brian Lara – the best left-hander in the world – tore into Murali as he racked up 688 runs in three games, in the last of which Murali took only three wickets for 231. When the sides next met two years later, Lara scored 209.

Murali's response was to develop a 'doosra', an off-spinner's googly and a delivery patented by Pakistan's Saqlain Mushtaq in the 1990s. Murali worked on the ball during a

brief spell with Kent towards the end of the 2003 season and unleashed it on England later that year when they returned to Sri Lanka. In that series, won 1–0 by Sri Lanka, England's left-handers were much less effective and Murali took 26 wickets in three games.

Murali was a hugely successful bowler up to the point he added the doosra to his armoury, but this weapon made him even more lethal. Previously he had taken 459 wickets in 82 Tests at an average of 23.55; in 51 subsequent Tests, he added another 341 wickets at the lower average of 21.61 while, most eye-catchingly of all, his strike rate plunged from a wicket every 60 balls to one in every 48.

The doosra was a controversial delivery, not just when bowled by Murali but by most off-spinners who sought to emulate the success enjoyed by Saqlain and Murali himself. Many experts thought that no one could bowl this ball without flexing their arm beyond acceptable limits. It brought Murali under fresh scrutiny but tests established that even with this delivery he stayed within 15 degrees. The ICC has recently sought to clamp down on suspect actions, with an array of off-spinners reported, including Saeed Ajmal of Pakistan, the leading bowler of this type since Murali's retirement from Tests in 2010. It is understandable that Murali was going to inspire imitators, and a good thing that he does, even if it is unlikely there will ever be anyone quite like him again, but it is also important that the rules and regulations, into which so much effort has gone, are observed.

It is always intriguing to see someone of his ilk weave his magic and equally important that finger spinners are allowed to develop their skills to the acceptable limit to maintain a viable and necessary role in international cricket.

29. GLENN McGRATH

Australia 1993–2007

No fast bowler has taken more Test wickets than Glenn McGrath's 563. It is a remarkable tribute to both his physical stamina and his enduring skill. He did not have the express pace that made many fast bowlers so dangerous, nor did he move the ball extravagantly through the air, but he had a method that provided a superb blend of accuracy and aggression and was more than a match for most. Usually one of these two virtues is sacrificed in the cause of the other. McGrath got the balance just right.

I remember watching a young McGrath bowl at Brisbane in the first Test of the 1994–95 Ashes series, and he did not obviously stand out as a champion in the making. He ended the game without a wicket, though there weren't to be many occasions like that in the years to come (statistically, in fact, this was to be the worst Test of his career). He did not feature again until the final match at the WACA, where he took six wickets, but with so much attention being lavished on Shane Warne, the new sensation, he remained a rather anonymous figure. All that changed soon enough.

Comparisons were often made with Curtly Ambrose, with whom perhaps he had most in common among the top performers of the day. Both were tall – McGrath was a couple of inches shorter but at 6ft 5in certainly had enough height to bowl a decent bouncer and hit the splice – and both were accurate, but interestingly, although Ambrose had slightly the better economy rate, it was McGrath who possessed the better strike rate, suggesting he more consistently asked the

right questions of the batsman. Ambrose would have been pacier for sure but if there was one thing that McGrath demonstrated it was that there was a lot more to fast bowling than pace itself.

He himself reckoned that he could work out a batsman after watching him play six balls, and that no-nonsense predatory streak was perhaps what made him so effective. He also observed that one of the key factors in his success was not getting bored with putting the ball in the same spot again and again. Let the batsman get bored first, was his philosophy. It was a method that worked for him the world over, even in Asia where his record dwarfs those of many fast men. His grumpiness – and he could be spectacularly grumpy – was perhaps a sign that while he might control his bowling, controlling his temper as well was not always possible.

He had a beautifully economical action. He did have issues with his ankles in later years, and was out for about a year in 2003–04 to undergo surgery, but he rarely broke down and, remarkably, back scans showed almost no indications of wear and tear. Having grown up in the New South Wales outback, he got into regular cricket relatively late in life and this may have helped in this regard. Inevitably a lot of young fast bowlers play the game as their bodies are still growing, and this has a deleterious effect, but McGrath's body escaped such hardships. He was slim, too, so he never carried any excess pounds, which can also take its toll on the body.

Just occasionally, he lost the plot a little. One such time was at Headingley in 2001, when Mark Butcher scored 173 not out to take England to a surprise win, and McGrath gave him too much width outside off stump. He also did not bowl particularly well in the first Test of the 1997 Ashes series at Edgbaston when Nasser Hussain scored a double century and England won by a big margin. But it is worth noting that on both occasions McGrath came back strongly in the next game. At Lord's in 1997 he returned figures of eight for 38, the best by any visiting player on the ground. He often bowled well from the Pavilion End at Lord's, where the slope brought the ball back into the right-hander and only added to his difficulties.

If there was anything in the pitch, McGrath could be counted on to exploit it with the new ball but aggression at the start of the innings could give way to wonderful control if that was what was needed later, when Warne started to come into the game. McGrath and Warne must rank as one of the greatest of all bowling combinations – it goes without saying very different in what they did with the ball but similar in their versatility in being able to either attack or defend as the situation demanded. They were a captain's dream and they above all made Australia the dominant side they were, only needing a couple of decent support bowlers, which they were certainly able to summon up most of the time, so it was a side that wasn't often going to struggle to take 20 wickets.

Australia in fact won 71 and lost only 16 of the 104 Test matches McGrath and Warne played together. McGrath took 488 wickets in those 104 games at 21.38 each, and Warne 513 at 24.87, so it can hardly be said that McGrath was less influential with the ball. Perhaps it was significant that the two Tests England won in the epic 2005 Ashes occurred when this partnership was not operating, McGrath a rare absentee, having trodden on the ball during the warm-up ahead of the Edgbaston Test and suffering an elbow problem before Trent Bridge. England beat Australia only three times when McGrath and Warne were in harness.

McGrath enjoyed bowling against West Indies every bit as much as he did England. When he began they were still the team to beat, and his first big series came in the Caribbean in 1995 when Australia became the first team in 15 years to win a series against West Indies. His aggression sent as clear a message as any that the West Indian hegemony was coming to an end. He was also hugely influential when the teams met in Australia in 1996–97 for what was billed as a world championship of Test cricket – Australia won 3–2 – and back in the Caribbean in 1999 when he took 30 wickets in four matches as the sides drew 2–2. Just as he did with England's most dependable player Michael Atherton, McGrath fared better than perhaps any bowler in the world in keeping Brian Lara in check. However good the batsman was, McGrath found a way to deal with them.

He timed his departure well, too, leaving the game in 2007 a champion, shortly after Australia had regained the Ashes after a 5–0 whitewash and won a third straight World Cup. No one has taken more wickets at World Cups than he has, another measure of his special status.

28. ALLAN BORDER

Australia 1978–94

Allan Border was perhaps not the most elegant left-hander you will ever see but he was the most effective of his generation and the central figure in the regeneration of Australian cricket in the 1980s. He was a tremendous competitor, extremely brave during a period in which bravery was an essential quality against the dominant force of the era, the West Indies' awesome pace attack, and others besides, and totally unwilling to take a backward step. He took a few blows and shed some blood in the process, but never quailed. He scored two unbeaten centuries against England towards the end of the 1981 Ashes during which he batted for hour after hour with a broken finger on his left hand. It was a highly impressive act of discipline and determination, and he gave plenty more like that.

Border came into the Australia side during the Packer years – we first saw him towards the end of the 1978–79 Ashes tour which England won 5–1 and in his second game he played two fighting innings of 60 not out and 45 not out – and endured a lot of defeats in his early career, during which he often fought a lone hand. These experiences shaped his personality and ultimately the team he led. Australian cricket owes Border a great deal because he laid the foundations for the uninterrupted years of triumph that followed under Mark Taylor and Steve Waugh. He and I were opposing captains in the 1985 and 1989 Ashes series in England, and I saw two very different people. The sociable if still highly competitive character that led Australia the first time was replaced by someone whose reluctance to exchange pleasantries unsubtly masked his ruthless determination to put his Australian side back on top. He was palpably a different animal by then, and it worked. Australia were to win eight Ashes series in a row, the first three of them under Border. His side also came within two runs of beating the all-conquering West Indies in 1992–93 when West Indies had not lost a series since 1980. In the end, that prize came the way of Taylor, Border's immediate successor, two winters later.

He managed to transmit his enormous ability and courage to his players and in effect rebuild the team in his image. The story of Dean Jones batting with Border in searing heat

and humidity in Chennai during the tied Test match of 1987 illustrates the point as well as any, with Jones, who had scored about 170 at the time, pleading to leave the field because he was regularly being sick by the side of the pitch. Border told him he was 'a weak Victorian' – Border himself was from Sydney but played a lot of his cricket for Queensland – and instructed him to stay. Jones duly stayed and went on to score 210 before being taken to hospital suffering from exhaustion.

Australian cricket was conscious of its debt and in 2000 instituted the Allan Border Medal, which is awarded to the outstanding player of the season as judged by his peers.

When he took over the captaincy after Kim Hughes resigned in tears midway through a home series against West Indies in 1984–85, Border could only take the team up but it took a while for progress to manifest itself and even he came close to giving up on the project. Remarkably, through all the difficulties, he managed to maintain his own form. He averaged a fraction over 50 in the 63 Tests he played before becoming captain, and 50.94 in the 93 matches he captained. He did not miss a Test between 1979 and retiring in 1994, a run of 153 straight games.

Australia's renaissance under Border really began with the victory at the 1987 World Cup on the subcontinent when the team came through a series of tight finishes to lift the trophy. Border himself had a relatively quiet tournament until the final against England in Kolkata where he rounded off Australia's innings with a run-a-ball 31 and then, to general astonishment, dismissed the England captain Mike Gatting with his workaday left-arm spin, Gatting miscuing an attempted reverse sweep. It was a moment that turned the game and Australia ran out winners by seven runs.

It would be a mistake to label Border as simply an over-my-dead-body blocker. He may have adopted that approach in Tests when the situation demanded, but when it came to the one-day game he had all the gears and was a talented shot-maker. He played a brilliant innings against us in a one-dayer in front of a big crowd at Melbourne during England's 1982–83 tour. It was a rain-shortened game so we only played 37 overs a side and after we had got a decent enough score Australia juggled their order and sent in Border to open, which in itself said something about his abilities. The atmosphere was unbelievable and you could see Border almost double in size as he walked out, while it appeared to have the opposite effect on Norman Cowans, whose arm seemed to lose a couple of yards of pace. Border got Australia off to a flyer with a quick 50, and they went on to win the game. Several years later he produced even more fireworks in a Nehru Cup match against England in Hyderabad, smashing 84 off just 44 balls.

A few months before he retired Border overtook Sunil Gavaskar as the leading run-scorer in Test history, a position he held from 1993 until 2005 when Brian Lara passed him. When he stopped playing, Border held the Test records for most runs (11,174), most Tests (156) and most catches by an outfielder (156). He scored 2,052 of his runs against West Indies, a tally beaten only by Graham Gooch during the period from 1979 to 1994, with no one else close. He was also a fine player of spin and had an excellent record in Asia. He was not only a fine catcher but an excellent outfielder with a hard, straight throw honed from early baseball coaching.

27. WASIM AKRAM

Pakistan 1985–2002

It is indisputable that Wasim Akram is the greatest left-arm fast bowler there has been. At his peak there was no question that he had the speed to trouble the best but he also used the ball – new or old – with rare skill. For some reason really top-class left-arm pace men have been relatively scarce and only Chaminda Vaas of Sri Lanka, Zaheer Khan of India, and the Australians Mitchell Johnson and Alan Davidson have like Wasim taken more than 150 Test wickets. None can match Wasim's haul of 414, on top of which amazingly he took 502 wickets in one-day internationals, in both spheres at an average of 23. Every bit as much as the cleverest of wrist-spinners, he had magician's hands.

Wasim was outstanding because of his ability to swing the ball in either direction, by some distance and apparently at will. He could also use the old ball in a way few others had ever managed, what we know now as reverse swing. He bowled with real pace with the new ball, but would often keep his opening spell quite short, wait for the ball to be roughed up slightly, and then return. And that's what made him and Waqar Younis, his younger ally, so lethal. The traditional approach had been to use the new ball for swing and seam, but with the Pakistanis – starting with Imran Khan and Sarfraz Nawaz before Wasim and Waqar came on the scene – it was a very different game.

While there was nothing wrong with how Wasim and Waqar started an innings, certainly if the ball was going through they knew, and their opponents soon enough

came to know, that they were even more effective when the ball was older. Their opening spells therefore served as preparation for the more dangerous phase of the game, with them bowling a fair few bouncers with the express purpose of abrading the ball. Then, later, they would keep the ball pitched up, giving it a chance to swing in either direction. Reverse swing in their hands was an absolute phenomenon. There is probably an optimum speed for pure reverse and they had it, but whatever the full explanation – and there were claims from some quarters that the ball was illegally tampered with to accelerate the roughing-up process – they were the finest exponents of reverse swing, and to my mind Wasim was ahead of Waqar.

Wasim, 6ft 5in and strongly built, varied his angles brilliantly, going over the wicket and around as the situation demanded, and he had such a quick arm that it was doubly hard for anyone new to the crease to pick up an early sight of the ball (hence, perhaps, his record four international hat-tricks). He had various other idiosyncrasies which hardly helped matters for the batsman, such as running up behind the umpire before jumping out at the moment of delivery, and hiding the ball in his hand to prevent the batsman getting any clues as to which way it might swing.

Wasim was a tougher proposition than Waqar, I believe, because he moved the ball a little more in both directions, and with equal dexterity either way. Waqar tended to move the ball more into the right-hander and less away from him. Personally I was more troubled by left-arm pace-men and found it harder to line them up. Typically they'd try and take the ball away from a left-hander from an off-stump line, and someone like Wasim had the ability to then bring it back in, bringing stumps and pads into play.

When they had the old ball going as they wanted, Wasim

and Waqar had the power to trigger some remarkable batting collapses, some of which I witnessed at close quarters in the later stages of the 1992 Test series in England. At Headingley, I saw plenty of partners come and go as we slumped from 292 for two to 320 all out, Waqar causing most of the damage, while at The Oval we lost our last seven wickets for 25 in the first innings and five for 21 in the second, Wasim to the fore both times. Although we lost the series, we actually won the first of those two games, though not without difficulty as Wasim in particular made us fight for the 99 runs we needed in the final innings. He gave us nothing. I batted more than two hours for an unbeaten 31 and it was one of the toughest, most fraught passages of play I experienced.

Wasim had also got the better of England a few months earlier, with a man-of-the-match performance in the World Cup final in Melbourne. His late hitting for 33 off 19 balls ensured Pakistan a competitive total and he later took the crucial wickets of Ian Botham, Allan Lamb and Chris Lewis, two of them for ducks. As that game illustrated, he could be a more than useful batsman. While you would hardly back him to bat for your life, he could be suitably dangerous if the requirement was hitting the ball into the stands. He managed to hit a Test match double century against Zimbabwe pretty much doing that, hitting 12 sixes and 22 fours in an unbeaten 257 at Sheikhupura. A more creditable effort perhaps was a second-innings century in Adelaide with his side in trouble.

Wasim was largely uncoached until he got into the Pakistan side. He was discovered when he happened to bowl in the nets at Javed Miandad. Fast-tracked into the national squad at the age of 18 – and knowing so little about the world that he was unaware he would be paid! – he took ten wickets in his second Test match in Dunedin in 1985. His cricketing education was greatly accelerated by spending several seasons with Lancashire, whom he helped to win several one-day trophies.

Pakistan has rarely been free of confusion, controversy or allegations of corruption and Wasim's reputation was among those tarnished by the Qayyum report into match-fixing in Pakistan, published in 2000, which barred him from the national captaincy.

26. SUNIL GAVASKAR

India 1971–87

Another in a long line of prolific run-makers to come out of Mumbai, Sunil Gavaskar was a little man with immense talent and determination. He had a wonderful technique, wonderful balance and a wonderful eye for tracking and manoeuvring the ball. I played many matches against him, mainly Tests but also some games of lesser importance, and he approached them all in the exactly the same way. The MCC Bicentenary match at Lord's in 1987 was for some of us a festival fixture but for him it was an opportunity to finally score a hundred on the famous old ground – an opportunity he duly took (he scored 188 for good measure). I've seen him bat in charity matches and there on display was the same thoroughness as always. More than most, batsmen who open the innings cannot leave things to chance and Sunny certainly wasn't one to do that.

Perhaps the innings of his I remember most vividly was his double century at The Oval in 1979. His reputation was already made by that stage – this was his 20th three-figure score for India in his 50th Test match, an amazing record – but he had previously spared England's bowlers the worst punishment. But this was a performance that summed him up: India had been set 438 to win or more likely around four sessions to survive and although the pitch was still good we gave them little chance of escape. We were in for the rudest of shocks. With the help of Chetan Chauhan and Dilip Vengsarkar, he very nearly pulled off what would have been an incredible victory, and only thanks to the late intervention of Ian Botham did the game end in the tensest of draws. They did everything but win the game.

Gavaskar provided a template as to how to construct a long run-chase but then perhaps we should not have been surprised. Three years earlier he had played his part in India successfully chasing down what was then a record 406 to beat West Indies in Trinidad. He scored 102 and India won by six wickets with something to spare. Like many great players, he thought nothing of rewriting the record books.

Gavaskar is one of the shrewdest, most analytical men you will ever meet and one indication of how carefully he thought about things was the skullcap he chose to wear at a time when helmets were coming into the game but were not quite the things of comfort they later became. The early helmets could be unwieldy and as much an encumbrance as an aid. His solution was a moulded 'lid' that sat under his cap and protected the temples but did not hamper his vision. It was a slightly weird solution to the problem but it worked very well for him. He was of course small enough at 5ft 5in to duck out of the way of many short balls but that was only part of the challenge and his record against the fast bowlers was outstanding.

Gavaskar's performances against the West Indies formed the stuff of legend. In his very first Test series, aged 21, he took

774 runs off them in four matches at an average of 154.80 (a record for anyone in their first series). This included a single and a double century in the same game, the double century scored while suffering from severe toothache. On his next tour of the Caribbean in 1975–76 he scored two more centuries, including the one in the record run-chase mentioned above. When West Indies toured India in 1978–79, he plundered 732 runs in six matches. These were not against the strongest attacks – West Indies in the early 1970s did not possess quite such nasty fast bowlers as later and in 1978–79 most if not all of their best pace-men had defected to Kerry Packer. But they were at full strength when in 1983 he scored 147 against them in Guyana, 121 at Delhi and 236 not out in Chennai.

The Delhi innings showed another side to his personality. Having started shakily against Malcolm Marshall and Michael Holding, he decided his best course of action was attack and he raced to his hundred off just 94 balls. A few years earlier I'd seen him hit John Lever over long on for six in the first over of the innings before then batting in his conventional fashion. Perhaps it was this same contrariness that led him to bat slowly through a 60-over one-day innings during the 1975 World Cup because he did not believe India could win, and to attempt to lead his batting partner off the field after he had been given out to a questionable lbw decision at Melbourne in 1981.

He could be quirky for sure. When we opposed each other as captains on England's tour of India in 1984–85, he took the very odd decision to allow India's first innings in the third Test in Kolkata to meander into the fourth day. Had the pace been quicker, we could have been under more pressure, and it must have been something he regretted when we went on to win the series. He was unimpressed when at the rest day

press conference I said he'd already gone on too long and he dubbed me 'The Preacher'. It was a rare case of him getting something wrong, although as a captain he was perhaps too defensive. Once India went one-up against us on our previous tour in 1981–82 he was happy to sit on the lead, which resulted in some stultifying cricket, but India were by then without their great match-winning spin bowlers and the price of failure in Indian cricket was high (especially if that failure came against Pakistan, as he subsequently discovered).

Gavaskar retired having scored more runs (10,122) and more hundreds (34), and having played in more Tests (125) than anyone to that point. He was a cricketing deity long before Sachin Tendulkar came along; indeed, he advised and encouraged the young Tendulkar to believe that he was capable of breaking the records he himself had set (which he duly did). His legacy goes deeper than just the playing. Since retiring, he has remained a constant presence behind the scenes, involved with the Maharashtra Cricket Association in Mumbai and the Indian board, even being appointed the BCCI's temporary chief executive. He continues to influence the game hugely, as befits the stature of the man.

25. GRAEME POLLOCK

South Africa 1963–70

Graeme Pollock was an early hero of mine, the number 1 hero in fact. He never let me down. The first Test match I ever went to watch was the England–South Africa Test at Trent Bridge in 1965, taken there by my parents. I was eight years old and wouldn't confess to watching every ball because I had a bat and ball with me, which I needed to play with at the back of the stands as well, but Pollock, a left-hander as I was, made a hundred and it is an innings that has gone down in the annals for its quality. Colin Cowdrey also made a hundred in that game but Pollock's certainly made the bigger impression. He scored 125 runs out of 160 added while he was at the crease, out of a team total of 269, which is a measure of how much better than the rest he was.

The next time I saw him I was touring South Africa with a schools team around Christmas 1974 and we were treated to one day's first-class cricket as spectators at St George's Park, and again he got a hundred for Eastern Province. He smashed it everywhere. There was a distinct contrast in style with Barry Richards. Whereas Richards had a little gentle movement of the feet and was always nicely balanced and elegant, Pollock by then had adopted a very wide stance which didn't require much movement, just a transfer of weight. If the ball was pitched up, he would just lean into the drive with his big forearms – he was a tall man and very strong – and high grip on the bat. He preferred to play off the front foot but if it was pitched short, he would just sway back and smack it into the stands.

The third time I saw him bat was for an International XI in a one-day game at Jesmond during the early 1980s when I actually played with him, me by this stage an established England player while he must have been around 40 years of age. Needless to say he got another hundred and much to my delight we batted together for a short time before I was out for something rather less! What a thrill that was, just to be able to say, Hi, Graeme, it's an absolute honour to be on the same field.

Years later he played in some of the charity matches I

helped organise in Zimbabwe for a wildlife charity, SAVE, and again he got runs every time. Even at the age of 60 he would go into the nets and prepare simply because he always wanted to give himself the best chance to play well.

It was, of course, a personal tragedy for Graeme, as it was for the likes of Barry Richards and Mike Procter, that he should be denied the opportunity to play a full Test match career. At least in his case he played for long enough to demonstrate beyond argument just how great a batsman he was. In 23 Tests spanning six series he scored 2,256 runs at an average of 60.97 that has only been beaten by Don Bradman, and he had clearly got a taste for the big time before he was cut off at the age of 26. Those figures do not lie. He was up against some high-quality bowlers in that period.

He scored a Currie Cup century at 16 but to a wide audience the first flowering of his genius came on South Africa's tour of Australia and New Zealand in 1963–64 when at the age of 19 he scored more than 1,000 runs in all matches, including five hundreds, and struck 122 and 175 in the third and fourth Tests. With his powerful stroke-play, he immediately became the player everyone wanted to watch. Perhaps only Sachin Tendulkar, who scored two Test centuries when he toured there in 1991–92 at the age of 18, has ever created such a big impression on a first visit to Australia as a young man.

Many brilliant performances followed. A few months before I first saw him at Trent Bridge, he scored a third Test century before turning 21 in his home city of Port Elizabeth against England (he might have added a fourth in the second innings of the same game but his captain declared with him on 77 not out); but it was Australia's bowling to which he took special liking. South African cricket touched rare heights during Australia's tours of 1966–67 and 1969–70 – they romped away 3–1 winners in the first, followed by a 4–0 whitewash in the second – but Graeme Pollock was the absolute star (his fast bowling brother Peter, father of Shaun, was another key member of the side). He scored a sublime double century in each series, 209 (out of a total of 353) in Cape Town over New Year in 1967 and 274 at Durban in February 1970 in what was then the highest innings ever played for South Africa. But by the following month he had, it transpired, played his last Test match.

Of course, it was not immediately apparent that the ban on sporting contact with South Africa would prove so permanent. Pollock played for the Rest of the World teams that initially filled in when tours of England and Australia were cancelled, scoring hundreds both times, but as the reality of the situation sank in, his form with the bat did fall away. He soon rallied, though, finding motivation in dominating the Currie Cup with Eastern Province and, later, Transvaal. Somewhat surprisingly he declined offers to play county cricket but perhaps this at least meant that he never lost his appetite. He became the first batsman ever to score 200 in a limited-overs match and for eight seasons in a row between 1974 and 1982 he averaged more than 60 and he kept playing successfully until he finally retired at the age of 43, signing off with an unbeaten 63 in his last innings in a Currie Cup final.

Just how motivated he remained was evident from his performances against the various rebel touring sides that went to South Africa during the 1980s. He may have been in his 40s but he not only wanted to play but to dominate, and that is what he did. He missed out against the English side that went in 1981–82 but he scored at least one hundred against every subsequent visiting team, and these contained some decent bowlers such as Sylvester Clarke, Franklyn Stephenson, Rodney Hogg and Terry Alderman.

24. RICHARD HADLEE

New Zealand 1973–90

It says a lot for how good Richard Hadlee was that he bore fair comparison as a fast bowler with first Dennis Lillee in the late 1970s and early '80s, and then Malcolm Marshall in the mid- to late '80s. He was not as quick as either but that did not greatly matter. What did was that he had much less impressive back-up. Hadlee, in essence, was the New Zealand bowling attack through the great part of his career. He was markedly better than anyone else in the team and he was the one who was going to get you out. He was the danger. If he had a good day his side were in the game, if he didn't they were not. It was not like that if you played Australia or West Indies.

It is to Hadlee's immense credit how competitive New Zealand became. They had some reliable batsmen, and one batsman of near-genius in Martin Crowe, and were well led for a long time by Geoff Howarth, but broadly speaking it was Hadlee who delivered the victories. When England were beaten for the first time in 48 years at Wellington in 1978, Hadlee cut them apart with figures of six for 26. When England were beaten in a series for the first time, in New Zealand in 1983–84, and then again in England in 1986 (series in which I was on the receiving end), he was the star bowler in the games his side won at Christchurch and Trent Bridge. He was also central to events when New Zealand won their first series against West Indies (1979–80), India (1980–81) and Australia (both home and away in 1985–86). The victories over Australia were especially memorable as

Australia paid a heavy price for preparing juicy surfaces at Brisbane and Perth and saw Hadlee make much better use of conditions than their own players. His first-innings figures at the Gabba of nine for 52, and match figures of 15 for 123, are the best for New Zealand in all Tests. In six matches, Hadlee claimed a staggering 49 wickets at 16.08. The Australians had no answer to him.

His great strength was hitting the right length and hitting the seam. He gave away very little. He generated a little bit of curve through the air but the main challenge was that he was going to keep bowling a length, keep you coming forward, then bowl you a bouncer which would be sharp in pace, just to stop you taking liberties, or to change the rhythm a bit. I confess he hit me on the head more than most, mostly when I wasn't wearing a helmet, which amply demonstrates that he could be more than quick enough when it suited him! In those days, at least against anyone but the West Indies, you might wear a helmet while playing yourself in, then take it off as you felt more comfortable. I did this once against New Zealand in a Test at The Oval, and Hadlee clearly took exception to me strolling out after tea without headgear. He sent down a string of bouncers, one of which struck me a glancing blow on the head. He'd made his point.

Although he moved the ball more through seam than swing, he could indeed swing it. In that match at Christchurch in 1983–84 I found myself severely embarrassed, deciding on seeing the ball leaving his hand that this was one to leave only to realise when the ball was halfway down that it was now swinging in nicely. Bad decision. It was an lbw that a blind man could have given on the certainty of the appeal alone!

He possessed a fine flowing action. In his early days, before I really came across him, he came in on a very long run but his bowling was rather wild in those days and he took the

decision to cut it down and concentrate on control. In his pomp, the run-up was shorter but he had such wonderful rhythm and such a wonderfully whippy action that he continued to generate more than enough pace. I never faced Shaun Pollock, of course, but I imagine he and Hadlee were very similar bowlers: not out-and-out quick but capable of something lively enough when it was needed.

Hadlee regularly out-bowled not only his colleagues but the opposition too. Fighting what must have felt like so many solitary battles may have contributed to his rather moody demeanour. He seemed a man apart, always very driven but working to targets of his own devising as well as team goals.

One of his most impressive achievements was the double of 1,000 runs and 100 wickets for Nottinghamshire in 1984, a feat that had not been performed for many years. He had joined Notts in 1978, helped them win their first championship for more than half a century in 1981, his own contribution being 745 runs and 105 wickets, and continued to give great service until 1987 when the county won another championship as well as the NatWest Trophy. He and Clive Rice, his captain and new-ball partner, proved deadly on some tailor-made green tops at Trent Bridge – balls used to come through at some interesting heights, I remember – but they were scarcely less effective away from home. Like Marshall, Hadlee did well to be so potent in county cricket while sustaining a long international career.

Hadlee developed into a dangerous lower-order batsman, especially in one-dayers, but one got the impression that without the advent of helmets he would have remained a less potent force with the bat. He did little with the bat in his early days and Ian Botham regarded him as his rabbit on New Zealand's 1978 tour. Within a couple of years, however, he had hoisted his batting average the right side of 20 and transformed himself into quite a capable practitioner. In fact, among his two Test centuries was one against West Indies. He rarely ventured higher than number 7, though.

Durable to the last, Hadlee was 39 years old when he played his final Tests in England in 1990, by which time he was the world's leading Test wicket-taker (a record he took from Botham and which was taken from him by Kapil Dev) and already a knight of the realm.

23. ANDY ROBERTS

West Indies 1974–83

Andy Roberts was godfather to the modern generation of West Indies fast bowlers. He came from what was at the time the cricketing backwater of Antigua, a Caribbean island that had not previously produced a Test cricketer, and established himself at the very top of the tree. He created genuine fear around the shires in his early seasons with Hampshire – as a youngster, I remember seasoned county players talking of his pace in awed tones – and although he lost his place in the West Indies side a couple of times towards the end of his career, he fought off the high-class competition and got it back again. When he did play, he always took the new ball and almost always bowled the first over of the innings, such was the reverence with which he was regarded by his colleagues. To them he was the 'Professor'.

Michael Holding, who opened the bowling with him many times, gives Roberts immense credit for leading the attack both on and off the field. Roberts understood the

intricacies of bowling fast better than the others. Many people were inclined to ascribe limited intelligence to fast bowlers, and assert that their muscles moved faster than their brains, but Roberts confounded such prejudices. He employed tricks that were not then widely known, such as deploying two bouncers of subtly different pace, a slow one then a deceptively quicker one designed to take the batsman by surprise, and holding the ball cross-seam. Dennis Lillee described him as the most complete fast bowler he saw at the time. But the basis of his game, at least in the early years, was some serious pace.

It is hard now to convey the impact Roberts made when he burst on to the scene in the early 1970s. He had played his first match for Hampshire – ironically against a touring West Indies side – in 1973 and made his Test debut against Mike Denness's England in the Caribbean the following winter but he was largely unknown when he began his first championship season in 1974. Not for long. Word soon got around about the havoc he was causing. This was of course before the arrival of helmets and the consequent stiffer resolve such protection induced in some players. That year Roberts took 119 wickets in the county championship at the exceptionally low average of 13.62 and unsurprisingly Hampshire carried off the title.

From England, Roberts went on to a Test tour of India where he created similar panic among the opposition. He took 32 wickets in the series, which was then a record for any visiting bowler in India and has only been beaten once since (by Malcolm Marshall, who in 1983–84 took 33 wickets in six games, one more than Roberts played). In England in 1976, and now with the rapidly improving Holding in harness as his new-ball partner, he took 28 wickets in five Tests, including ten in the match at Lord's and nine at Old

Trafford. During that series he reached 100 Test wickets in just his 19th match; only five bowlers have ever got there faster and none of them was a bowler of genuine pace.

I first encountered his bowling on that 1976 tour in one of my earliest matches for Leicestershire. I scored 89 unbeaten in the second innings but it was a very flat Grace Road pitch and he was naturally saving himself for the Test matches. I later faced him in a Test match at Trent Bridge in 1980 which went better for him than it did for me: he took eight wickets in the game – I was caught at slip off him in the first innings for not many – and saw his side home with the bat in a tight finish, although not before I had dropped him, much to the chagrin of my captain, Ian Botham. I did not feature again in the series but we crossed paths subsequently in the Caribbean the next year. That time, he was the one who lost the support of the selectors after going wicketless in Antigua, prompting speculation – misplaced as it proved – that his international career might be over.

He was always a quietly spoken guy and there were no histrionics on the field. Forget sledging. What you got from Andy was a withering look. Then he went back to his mark, perhaps making a small change to his field before trying to get you out again.

Soon after that tour, I got to observe him from much closer quarters when he joined us at Leicestershire. He had stopped playing for Hampshire in 1978 to lighten his workload but now that he was playing a little less often for West Indies he was ready for a fresh challenge. He was hardly garrulous in the dressing room either but he was measured in what he did say and was worth listening to. On the field, he would have a quick word with his captain, as though to say, 'This is what we need to do.' He worked things out very quickly and in composed fashion. He didn't drink and we would not see much of him during away games. He would eat his food early and go to bed.

If the decision to join us was designed to rejuvenate his game, it certainly worked. He bowled superbly for us in 1982, almost getting back to the pace he routinely generated in the mid-1970s, and taking 54 wickets at 19.01. Indeed, he nearly took us to the championship. With two games to go we were only two points behind Middlesex, the eventual champions, and it was not his fault we lost our way in the last two games against Notts and Kent. He continued this vein of form in the Caribbean the following winter when he was the pick of the West Indies bowlers once again, taking 24 wickets in five Tests against India.

Tall and strong, Roberts proved highly durable. He was the first West Indies out-and-out fast bowler to take 200 Test wickets, and played more first-class matches, and took more first-class wickets (889 at 21.01 each), than Holding, Colin Croft or Joel Garner.

22. BILL O'REILLY

Australia 1932–46

Bill O'Reilly's Test career was quite short – circumstances conspired against his early recognition as a major talent and the Second World War effectively cut him off from international cricket at the age of only 32 – but he nevertheless made an unforgettable impact.

Don Bradman, who played against him in state cricket and alongside him in most of his Test matches, said O'Reilly was the best bowler he ever faced and the best bowler he ever saw. Wally Hammond, who opposed him in all 19 of the Tests he played against England, said O'Reilly made the ball jump off the pitch better than any other slow bowler he had met. O'Reilly's height was a key factor in his success; at 6ft 1in, he was tall for a spin bowler and approached the wicket with a bounding run. He possessed the build and temperament of a fast bowler, his ultra-aggressive manner taking aback opponents and teammates alike, and earning him the nickname of 'Tiger'. Every ball he bowled was charged with hostility and he had an appeal that could make batsmen jump out of their skin. 'Hitting Bill O'Reilly for four was like disturbing a hive of bees,' Bradman said.

O'Reilly's sheer unorthodoxy was one of the reasons why some people were slow to believe in him. He gripped the ball in unusual fashion and rejected the received wisdom that a leg-spinner should bowl to an array of close catchers on the leg side, preferring to target the stumps. In his way, he challenged perceptions about leg-spin bowling every bit as much as Shane Warne did later. When O'Reilly died in 1992, *Wisden* among others hailed him as the greatest spin bowler the game had produced. As it happened, that was the year that Warne, who must be considered his greatest rival for that title, made his debut for Australia.

Although they did not oppose each other often in first-class cricket – they played together for New South Wales before Bradman moved to South Australia – O'Reilly dismissed Bradman six times and also, on one famous occasion during a testimonial match in Sydney in which Bradman had been due to bat at number 3 but O'Reilly was bowling a devastating spell, prompted him to drop himself three places down the order (Bradman went on to score a double century). O'Reilly also had an excellent record against Hammond, England's

leading batsmen, whom he dismissed seven times for scores of 26 or fewer.

Test cricket was a batsman's game in the 1930s – timeless matches in Australia, featherbed pitches there and often in England too – and it is in this context that bowling records have to be assessed. Taking into account the one Test he played for Australia straight after the Second World War, O'Reilly's figures of 144 wickets in 27 Tests at 22.59 bear comparison with anyone else's during this period. Only Clarrie Grimmett, his leg-spinning ally in the Australia team, and Maurice Tate of England took more wickets, both at higher averages; Hedley Verity, England's left-arm spinner, also took 144 wickets but again at a higher average. In Ashes Tests, only Grimmett, with 106 wickets to O'Reilly's 102, took more wickets and he bowled many more overs and averaged 32.44 whereas O'Reilly's figure was 25.36, remarkably low considering the conditions.

O'Reilly could bowl well on any sort of pitch. It has always been reckoned that the English climate and English surfaces don't favour leg-spinners but O'Reilly (and Warne) blew sizeable holes in that argument. O'Reilly was superb in England on his two tours, taking more than 100 wickets both times at around 17 runs apiece, while in the Tests he captured 28 wickets in 1934 and 22 in 1938 (when only four matches were played due to rain washing out the game in Manchester). He was the leading wicket-taker on either side on both occasions, and played a starring role in two of the three matches Australia won. In the first Test at Trent Bridge in 1934, he bowled his side to victory with only ten minutes left on the clock on the final day with figures of seven for 54; at Headingley in 1938, he took 10 for 122 in the match, his victims including Hammond in both innings, the second time for a first-ball duck courtesy of a googly. When there really was nothing in the pitch, he could contain better than almost anyone: at The Oval in 1938, when Hutton made his 364 in an England total of 903 for seven, O'Reilly still managed to wheel down 85 overs for only 178 runs.

O'Reilly took more than 20 wickets in each of the five full series he played, four against England, one against South Africa. His part in the 1932–33 Ashes series has largely been forgotten because of the controversy over England's Bodyline tactics and the fact England won 4–1, but O'Reilly's contribution was immense. He took ten wickets in the one game Australia won and got through an enormous amount of work, bowling 383.4 overs in the five matches while conceding fewer than 1.90 runs per over. It was a warning of what was to come.

O'Reilly bowled with a lot of variety. His leg-break was a big weapon – Bradman said it was hard to imagine anyone could bowl a nastier one – but he also possessed top-spinners and googlies, plus a vicious faster ball. England's Maurice Leyland said the first over he received from O'Reilly – which was in the days of eight-ball overs in Australia – contained eight different deliveries.

O'Reilly grew up in rural New South Wales. He moved to Sydney at the age of 18 to follow his father into teaching and there began a remarkable career in grade cricket that would see him take almost 1,000 wickets at an average of 9.44. He failed a state trial when he was 20 but played three games for the state in 1927–28, when he turned 22. Unfortunately teaching then took him away from the city again for three years – during which he developed his googly – and he did not establish himself in the NSW side until 1931–32 after taking five wickets, including that of Australia captain Bill Woodfull, in his second match of the season.

Within weeks, he was playing for Australia and bowling

81.4 overs on his first appearance. During that match, he failed to appeal for lbw and the umpire later informed him that had he appealed he would have given the batsman out. O'Reilly made sure he didn't make that mistake again.

21. KEITH MILLER

Australia 1946–56

If the sole criterion of this list were glamour, Keith Miller might have come out number 1. He did the things that make cricket most interesting to the masses – bowled fast, hit the ball huge distances, held stunning reflex catches – while also possessing Hollywood looks and an unquenchable sense of fun. Having survived Second World War service as a fighter pilot, he wasn't prepared to take anything too seriously and that only served to imbue his cricket with even more zest. Alan Davidson, a fine all-rounder in his own right and among a generation of Australian players who idolised Miller, rated him along with Garry Sobers as the best all-rounder who ever lived. He is certainly Australia's best.

Miller could turn a match with an impromptu passage of star-sprinkled play, such as when he bowled out South Australia for 27 having arrived late at the ground as the players were taking the field. He took seven for 12. The bare statistics of the game, though, meant little to him, and scarcely did justice to his talents, but his figures were nevertheless hugely impressive. He was the second all-rounder after Wilfred Rhodes to complete the Test double of 2,000 runs and 100 wickets – a feat so much harder to do in the days when there was so much less Test cricket – and the difference between his batting average (36.97) and bowling average (22.97) was significantly in credit, to an extent matched only by Sobers, Jacques Kallis and Imran Khan.

Miller's fast bowling partnership with Ray Lindwall ranks among the game's most iconic. They were the scourge of England's batsmen in the immediate post-war period: 34 wickets between them in 1947–48, another 40 in 1948 and 32 in 1950–51, all three series emphatically won by Australia, and although England then won the next three series, the two of them remained potent weapons. Denis Compton said their bowling at Lord's in 1953 was the fastest he faced and they were said to be still very quick when Australia toured the Caribbean in 1955. Miller had left England in 1953 with predictions that he was finished as a fast bowler ringing in his ears but he actually enjoyed his biggest haul of 21 wickets when he returned for his final tour of England in 1956 in a series of few other highlights for the Australians as Jim Laker made fools of them, no one more so than Miller himself (he was out to Laker six times).

Fielding sides were entitled to a new ball much earlier in those days – amazingly, after just 55 overs in 1948 – which only played into the hands of this formidable pairing. They induced just as much trepidation in other sides, especially Miller, who stood more upright in his action than Lindwall and was capable of making the ball lift alarmingly. Miller was not averse to making liberal use of the short ball and attracted plenty of criticism as a result. He was once roundly booed by the Nottingham crowd for subjecting Len Hutton to one such barrage, and the following day knocked Denis Compton, a kindred spirit and good friend, back on to his stumps to end a fighting innings of 184, but he possessed

charm enough to ensure that the hostility did not last. His bowling in any case was not unrelentingly hostile: he would vary the searing pace with an assortment of leg-breaks, off-breaks or googlies, which broke the boredom and often caught out an unwitting batsman.

Miller was a substantial batsman, good enough to play the vast majority of his Test innings at number 3, 4 or 5, higher than most genuine all-rounders would be capable of doing. He scored four of his seven hundreds against West Indies, who were an emergent force in the early 1950s, and whose tour of Australia in 1951–52 was given world championship billing. Miller contributed 362 runs and 20 wickets to that series and 439 runs and 20 wickets in the Caribbean in 1955.

Perhaps his finest innings was the century he scored at Lord's in 1953 that created the opportunity for an Australian win so famously thwarted by Willie Watson and Trevor Bailey on the last day. England ultimately won that series but English satisfaction in the discovery of a fast bowler of their own in Fred Trueman was tempered by the mauling Trueman received at Miller's hands in the final match of the tour, Miller scoring 262 in a day.

Miller, who loved to gamble on the horses and life in general, was not inclined to take the safe course and in political terms this might have cost him dear. He was never made Australia captain even though he successfully led New South Wales, was a natural leader of men and was the most obvious to take over from Lindsay Hassett in 1953. For this, Don Bradman was widely held to be responsible, and Miller certainly didn't share 'The Don's' ruthlessly unsentimental approach to playing the game. Bradman was reportedly unimpressed by Miller's decision to give his wicket away first ball during the Australian massacre of Essex's bowling at Southend in 1948, when they racked up 721 in a day. Shortly after the tour Miller bowled bouncers at the great man during Bradman's testimonial match. Bradman was also reckoned to have used his influence as an Australian board member to expedite Miller's omission from a tour of South Africa, although an injury to another player meant that in the end Miller did go (fully justifying his presence with 246 runs and 17 wickets in the Tests). All this only added to the impression of Miller as a cricketing rebel, the shiniest of loose cannons.

Miller made a mark in state cricket before the outbreak of war – he scored 181 on his NSW debut at the age of 18 – but was effectively denied a start to his cricketing career proper until the age of 25. He kept his cricket going between sorties during the war though, and was perhaps the outstanding star of the Australian Services side that entertained crowds in England and India in 1945. In one match at Lord's he hit a six on to the top tier of the pavilion. The brand of cricket he played in the 'Victory Tests' against England was the brand he stuck to, and it won him the hearts of millions.

20. DENIS COMPTON

England 1937–57

Denis Compton was as glamorous a cricketer as England have ever possessed. He played in a style that captivated the crowds, last-second sweeps blending with sumptuous cover drives, and there was a devil-may-care attitude to everything he did that meant he was not someone to take your eye off. He rose fast, unknown one minute, scoring runs for England against Australia the next when only a few days past his 20th birthday. Until he developed a chronic knee problem in his early 30s as a result of a parallel career as a winger with Arsenal, he never really struggled and perhaps as a result never really lost the boyish enthusiasm that suggested he thought everything was just a lark. But by then, he was already the nation's darling following his feats in the years immediately after the Second World War, when his batting touched a sublime peak and sport was providing the masses with the perfect antidote to the miseries of war.

If all that was not enough, Compton was handsome too, with an unruly mop of black hair tamed with Brylcreem, but he exhibited the kind of flaws that suggested he was perhaps not really that different from the man in the street. His running between the wickets was chaotic and his time-keeping atrocious. The stories one has heard of him arriving at Lord's in his dinner jacket after a night on the tiles and scoring hundreds with borrowed bats can only appeal.

He, like others, missed out on some of his best years to the war but that at least meant he was hungry for the game and had reached full maturity when peace finally came. His achievements for Middlesex and England in the late 1940s, and the long hot summer of 1947 in particular, when he smashed so many records, are the stuff of legend. That his friend and teammate Bill Edrich was also in stupendous form at the same time, and also well worth watching, only added to the attraction: it must have seemed like a racing certainty that one or other, and possibly both, would come off on any given day.

No one ever measured Compton by figures alone but the figures say a lot about his dominance during this golden time. In the 1946 season, he scored more runs and more hundreds than any other player (2,403 runs, ten hundreds);

in 1947, he again scored more runs and more hundreds than anyone, not only in that season but in any season before or since (3,816 runs and 18 hundreds); in 1948, only Len Hutton did better than Compton's 2,451 runs and nine hundreds; and in 1949, his tallies of 2,530 runs and nine hundreds were eclipsed only by Hutton and James Langridge. In the winter of 1946–47 he toured Australia and New Zealand, and in 1948–49 South Africa, and on each occasion was again the leading batsman in terms of both runs and centuries. In an up-country match on the South Africa tour he scored a triple century in just 181 minutes, which remains the fastest on record.

For England he was, along with Hutton, one of the two best batsmen in the side. Between 1946 and 1949, he scored 11 hundreds in the space of 20 Tests, four against Australia, five against South Africa and two against New Zealand. The 753 runs he scored in the series with South Africa in 1947 still stands as the record for an England batsman in a home series. His duels with Ray Lindwall and Keith Miller formed part of the folklore of the period, and initially at least he probably had the better of things. Although his instinct was to play extravagantly, and take more risks than Hutton would have countenanced, his ability to score runs against Lindwall and Miller showed how good his defence must have been. He certainly applied himself when he scored twin centuries to earn England a draw in Adelaide in 1946–47. At Old Trafford in 1948 he was forced to retire early in his innings after edging a ball from Lindwall on to his head but he returned – possibly strengthened by a brandy or two – at 119 for five to score a sparkling 145 not out and hoist his side to 363. How appropriate that the man of the series award in Ashes Tests is now called the Compton–Miller medal.

The onset of knee trouble in 1949 resulted in surgery the

following year and was a contributory factor in Compton's wretched series in Australia in 1950–51 when he mustered just 53 runs in his eight innings, a salutary reminder that even the greatest can struggle badly at times. He had been appointed vice-captain for that tour, the first modern professional to be given the post and a step that paved the way to Hutton's subsequent appointment to the full captaincy. After that, Compton did not quite so consistently touch the heights of old, and never hit another hundred against Australia, but he nevertheless enjoyed some special moments. He hit the winning runs at The Oval in 1953 when the Ashes were regained for the first time in 19 years and in 1954 batted less than five hours in scoring 278 against Pakistan at Trent Bridge.

In 1952, he scored his 100th hundred in first-class cricket, and took fewer innings to do so than any other player apart from Don Bradman. That, and the fact he averaged more than 50 in both first-class cricket and Tests, should prove beyond all doubt that his technique was much sounder than his popular reputation as a dasher would suggest.

So obvious were Compton's talents that he joined Middlesex and Arsenal when he left school at 14. He scored 1,000 runs in the year of his county debut, at 18 the youngest ever to do so, and the following year when he scored 65 in his first match for England he only narrowly failed to top 2,000 runs. In 1938, he scored 102 in his first Test against Australia – at 20 years 19 days he remains the youngest to score a century for England – and in the next match saved the game with an unbeaten 76. Nor were his footballing achievements insignificant. He won league and cup with Arsenal and played wartime internationals for England. It seems remarkable now that anyone could combine serious careers in cricket and football at the same time but Compton managed it for many years, although his football did sometimes prevent him touring with England in the winter. The quick feet he needed for football must have helped his batting.

It should also be remembered that Compton was a very useful left-arm wrist spinner who took more than 600 first-class wickets, including 73 in his amazing summer of 1947! He also handed down good cricketing genes, his grandson Nick also playing Test matches for England.

19. RICHIE BENAUD

Australia, 1952–64

Richie Benaud displayed flair in everything he did, whether it was aggressive batting, intelligent and varied leg-spin, brilliant close catching, instinctive and positive captaincy or insightful TV commentary, which is probably what most people, too young to have seen him play for Australia, know him for. He has been famous for more than 60 years and what underpinned everything with him throughout that time was a deep love and understanding of the game.

If he were to be remembered for just one thing, it perhaps ought to be leadership. He more than anyone led Australian cricket out of the doldrums in the late 1950s – with his all-round cricket before he formally took over the national captaincy in 1958 – and he, along with his opposite number Sir Frank Worrell, did a great deal to revive general interest in Test cricket with the bold way they conducted what turned into a truly epic series between Australia and West Indies in 1960–61. That series began with the celebrated

tied Test in Brisbane in which Benaud's run-out for 52 with seven runs needed proved a major turning point during the game's climax.

Tactically he was razor sharp, while never losing sight of the fact that a captain could realistically only hope to control so much of what happened during the course of a game spanning several days and many hours. One of his most famous sayings was: 'Captaincy is 90 per cent luck and 10 per cent skill. But don't try it without the 10 per cent.' He certainly had that 10 per cent and, like Mike Brearley, appeared to possess the uncanny knock of creating his own good fortune, probably by being so good at anticipating what might happen next.

If conjuring victory from defeat in the 1981 Ashes was Brearley's defining achievement, Benaud's finest hour was a not dissimilar Houdini-like act at Old Trafford 20 years earlier, only a few months after the historic contests with Worrell's team. Then, with the series standing 1–1 after three matches and England 150 for one needing only a further 106 to take a 2–1 lead, he chose to forget that he was handicapped by a shoulder injury and, operating from round the wicket and into the rough, bowled his country to victory with a spell of five for 12 from 25 balls, thereby retaining the Ashes. If Brearley can claim to be England's finest captain of all time, the same status might be accorded Benaud among Australian leaders.

Inspired to bowl leg-spin by watching Clarrie Grimmett, Benaud first played for New South Wales at the age of 18 and for Australia at 21 but it took him time to fulfil his talents at the highest level. He smashed a maiden Test hundred in just 78 minutes in Jamaica in 1955 but the circumstances were hardly the most taxing – six other centuries were scored in the same game – and it took him 25 matches to record his first five-for. He also tasted a fair bit of defeat in his early years, finishing on the losing side to England in three straight Ashes series. English conditions were hardly conducive to leg-spin and he made little impression with the ball on the 1953 and 1956 tours (even accounting for his Manchester triumph in 1961 his Test wickets in England cost almost 40 apiece).

Then things clicked on a tour of the subcontinent that followed straight on from the 1956 tour. Australia lost to Pakistan on a matting wicket in Karachi but Benaud then proved the decisive player with 23 wickets in three Tests in India in a series Australia won 2–0. A year later he produced what ranks among the finest all-round performances of all time in South Africa, where in five matches he scored 329 runs and took 31 wickets. Only two other players – George Giffen and Ian Botham – have ever scored 300 runs and taken 30 wickets in the same series. Australia won that series 3–0 and on the tour as a whole Benaud's return in all first-class matches was a stupendous 817 runs and 106 wickets. When Ian Craig fell ill, Benaud was the natural choice to take over the captaincy against England in 1958–59.

He took to the promotion effortlessly. England were trounced 4–0 and if the methods of Benaud's pace attack were questioned – this was at the height of the 'throwing' controversy – his own bowling was beyond reproach and he was leading wicket-taker on either side with 31 at 18.83. A year later Australia toured Pakistan and India again and this time won both series and Benaud was again the star with 47 wickets in the eight Tests at 20.19. Then came the tight victories, both by 2–1 margins, over West Indies and England.

With his shoulder problem causing him increasing difficulty, his effectiveness as a bowler began to diminish but he nevertheless retained the Ashes at home in 1962–63 with a 1–1 draw. He played one more series, at home to South Africa in 1963–64, initially as captain but then under Bob Simpson, before retiring from all cricket at the age of just 33.

If that was sad, the story of the second, triumphant phase of his Australia career was not. During it, he averaged five more points with the bat than he had earlier, and nine points fewer with the ball, while Australia won 19 Tests and lost only five. At the time of his retirement, Benaud had taken 248 wickets in Tests, more than anyone else for Australia up to that point and second only to Fred Trueman among all nations. He had also captured a record 266 wickets for New South Wales. He had a whole bag of tricks – googlies, flippers and top-spinners, countless variations in flight – and was very accurate by the standards of his breed.

My entire experience of Richie is of him as a broadcaster, first listening to him and then, in my early days behind the microphone, working alongside him in the commentary box for Channel Nine and the BBC. For me, he was and is the guru of cricket commentary. His choice of words and manner of delivery were always pitch-perfect. To a novice such as myself, he was generous of spirit, always happy to talk and pass on advice. It is easy in our business to fire from the hip but one of his great aphorisms is 'Engage brain first before speaking' and he was always very careful to avoid making sweeping statements about issues that might develop and force some revision.

His influence extended into many areas. He was a key adviser to Kerry Packer during World Series Cricket, a groundbreaking venture that was highly controversial at the time but for which all well-remunerated modern cricketers should be thankful. Taking together his contributions on and off the field, he must rank as one of the most significant cricketing figures of all time.

18. WILFRED RHODES

England 1899–1930

Wilfred Rhodes touched rare heights as an all-rounder. In Test matches, he had two distinct phases: the first as a slow left-armer, probably the most skilful in the game to that point; the second as a batsman good enough to open the innings alongside Jack Hobbs against Australia. At Melbourne in 1904, he bowled England to victory on a rain-affected pitch with 15 wickets for 124 runs, match figures that were then the best on record in Ashes Tests; eight years later, on the same ground, he shared in an opening stand of 323 with Hobbs that has only ever been beaten once for England, his own contribution being 179.

He took more than half his 127 Test wickets between 1899 and 1904, and scored more than half his 2,325 Test runs between 1909 and 1914, but for Yorkshire he remained steadfastly effective with bat and ball for years on end, and was a major factor in the 12 championships they won during his time. No one has ever matched his haul of 16 season's doubles of 1,000 runs and 100 wickets. His career tally of 39,802 runs and 4,187 wickets puts him on a par with WG Grace and his long-time teammate and ally, George Hirst, both of whom also topped 35,000 runs and 2,500 wickets. Hirst famously also hailed from the Yorkshire village of Kirkheaton, also batted right-handed and bowled left-arm, although in his case fast-medium swing. Hirst, six years the elder, proved less successful in Test cricket than Rhodes, but they combined memorably on two occasions in 1902, bowling unchanged except for one over to dismiss Australia for 36 at Edgbaston (Rhodes seven for 17, Hirst three for 15), and as the last-wicket pair scoring the final 15 runs needed for victory at The Oval amid scenes of almost unbearable tension. Rhodes was then only 24 years of age but was already marked out, like Hirst, as a good man in a crisis.

It says much about the regard in which Rhodes was held that when England needed to pick a team to beat Australia at The Oval 24 years later they turned to him – chiefly as a bowler once again – even though he was by then 48 years of age. He was top of the national bowling averages at the time, and this would be the year of his 16th and last double, but even so he had not played a Test match for five years since being dropped after just one match of the 1921 series, seemingly for good. He did not let his side down, bowling immaculately in both innings and taking full advantage of a rain-affected pitch on what proved to be the final afternoon. His match analysis read 45 overs, 24 maidens, 79 runs, six wickets, and all six of his victims had Test centuries to their names. He subsequently played four further Tests on a tour of West Indies in 1930, making him at 52 the oldest man ever to play Test cricket, a record he still holds. By the time he finally stopped, no slow left-armer had ever taken more Test wickets and it was not until after the Second World War that anyone else managed the feat of 2,000 runs and 100 wickets in Tests.

Rhodes was only 20 when he was fast-tracked into the Yorkshire side after Lord Hawke famously jettisoned the county's incumbent left-arm spinner, Bobby Peel, for a disciplinary breach that may or may not have involved him urinating on the outfield at Sheffield (accounts vary). Even at that tender age, Rhodes was ready. He took six wickets in his first match against MCC, 13 for 45 on his championship debut against Somerset and ended his first season with a record 154 wickets. In his second season, 1899, he was chosen for three of the five Tests against Australia, taking seven wickets on his debut, and claimed 179 victims in all. In the three summers after that his hauls amounted to 261, 251 and 213, which even by the crowded county calendars of the day were significant returns. That amounts to 1,058 wickets in just five seasons, and his first five at that.

Short and solidly built, Rhodes operated off a short run-up and could wheel away for hours, probing at the batsman's patience with his unerring accuracy and his subtle variations in flight. He very rarely dropped short in length and proudly claimed in old age – he lived to a splendid 95 years of age, though he was blind for the last 21 – that he was never cut. He was near-impossible to play on a wet pitch but also very hard to get away on good ones. According to legend, the great Australian batsman Victor Trumper once exclaimed during a match at Sydney, 'For God's sake, Wilfred, give me a minute's rest.'

It says a lot about Rhodes that he set himself to improve so significantly as a batsman when his place with Yorkshire and England was assured as a bowler. He went in at number 10 or number 11 for England until in his first Test match in Australia in 1903–04 he put on 130 for the last wicket with RE Foster in the game at Sydney, in which Foster played a famous innings of 287 (this remained England's tenth-wicket record until it was beaten by Joe Root and James Anderson at Trent Bridge in 2014). He proved especially hard to shift on tour where the pitches were truer and the ball moved less; in those circumstances his defence was hard to breach. Accounts suggest that he was not the prettiest batsman to watch – he was one of the first to adopt an open-chested stance at the crease – but he could be mighty effective.

He was probably right to diversify because England

soon discovered an arguably even more talented, if more mercurial left-arm spinner in Colin Blythe. For a few years Blythe bowled many of the overs that had previously fallen to Rhodes, and after him Frank Woolley, another major all-rounder, bowled to good effect for England in the same style.

Rhodes typified Yorkshire cricket in the days of the amateur–professional divide. Yorkshire's teams were packed with wily pros and Rhodes was the wiliest of them all. He possessed enormous cricketing nous, knowing everything about pitches and opponents, and in his way did a lot for the reputation of the professional. He was co-opted on to the England selection panel along with Jack Hobbs and, like Hobbs, would have acted as an able lieutenant to various (always amateur) England captains. He also in his final days at Yorkshire acted as mentor to Hedley Verity, the next in a long line of great slow left-armers at the club.

17. LEN HUTTON

England 1937–55

There was a heroic dimension to Len Hutton's career that was not always evident even with some of England's other very great batsmen. He had talent in abundance all right – how else could he have scored a century in his second Test when only a few days past his 21st birthday, or set a world Test record score of 364 at the age of 22 against an Australia attack containing Bill O'Reilly and marshalled by Don Bradman? – but for much of his career England were not as strong a batting side as they had been when Jack Hobbs and Walter

Hammond reigned supreme. He took his responsibilities as seriously and soberly as that other imperturbable Yorkshire and England opener Herbert Sutcliffe. Not for him the extravagances of Denis Compton. When the captaincy came his way in 1952 – he was the first professional in the 20th century to be appointed to the post – the burden only grew. Yet he personally achieved great things, against some very great bowlers, and his team enjoyed a lot of success under him, including home and away Ashes wins.

Armed with an immaculate technique, Hutton was consistently England's best batsman against what was often a fiercely strong Australia side. He topped the averages in four of the six series he played against them and although he slipped to third place in the 1948 series below Compton and Cyril Washbrook – the only one of the many opening partners he had in Test cricket with whom he enjoyed sustained success – he nevertheless scored 342 runs in the four Tests he played (he was dropped for one match because the selectors suspected he was struggling to cope with Ray Lindwall and Keith Miller, something which subsequent events showed to be an exaggeration: he remained amazingly hard to shift). The one time he was not a major force with the bat was in Australia in 1954–55 when the strain of leading England to their first series win Down Under for 22 years took an immense toll; even so he scored some important runs at important times.

Before England regained the Ashes under him in the previous series in England in 1953 after an agonisingly long wait, Hutton had known little but defeat against Australia, but on the few occasions when they came away with a result he usually had something to do with it, most famously with his record-breaking score at The Oval in 1938. That was when his amazing powers of concentration first became apparent to the wider world: in a final match of the series played to a finish, he batted into the third day and by the time he was out after 797 minutes England were 770 for six and well on their way to victory. It remains the longest innings ever played for England. Although, of course, he never beat that effort he gave countless other displays of resilience when the pitch and the bowling – O'Reilly notwithstanding – had much more life in them than they did then. In the next 12 Tests he played against Lindwall and Miller after being dropped mid-series in 1948, he scored 1,208 runs and in the 1950–51 series in Australia stood head and shoulders above every other batsman on either side. While he scored 533 runs at an average of 88.83, his nearest rival in terms of average was Keith Miller with 350 runs at 43.75. He played one of the most celebrated of all innings seen on a 'sticky dog' in Brisbane, scoring 62 not out while only one other teammate managed to make it to double figures.

Hutton was also immense at the top of the order on the 1948–49 tour of South Africa when he scored 577 runs and Washbrook contributed 542 in a series England won 2–0, and he was even better in dealing with the great West Indies side that emerged shortly after the war. England collectively had little answer to the unanticipated wiles of Sonny Ramadhin and Alf Valentine in 1950 but Hutton was the first to articulate a response with an astonishing double century in the final match of the series at The Oval. Carrying his bat for 202 out of a team score of 344, he did not give a chance in almost eight hours. No other England batsman scored 50 in either innings. Four years later in the Caribbean, he almost single-handedly hauled England back from 2–0 down to earn a 2–2 draw with scores of 169 in Georgetown and 205 in Kingston. The two innings spanned 16 hours and again were chanceless.

If this paints a picture of a man of obstinate defiance, it was far from the complete picture. Hutton was one of the most handsome cover drivers the game has seen and before the outbreak of war in 1939 – an interruption that surely cost him many of his finest years – he was regarded by some in Yorkshire, where defence is held among the higher virtues, as something of a reckless dasher. Hutton himself reckoned he was then at his peak. Although he occasionally gave glimpses of his full repertoire of strokes after the war, he changed – in part because he felt he had to, Yorkshire as well as England not being quite the force they had been. This, however, did not satisfy the critics, who felt he was failing to do justice to his talent. There could be little arguing with the results though, as he churned out runs for county and country. His season's aggregate of 3,429 runs in 1949 has only been beaten by Compton and Bill Edrich in their famous summer of 1947 and Tom Hayward in 1906. As Trevor Bailey once said of Hutton, 'He only gambled on certainties'.

It is worth remembering too that Hutton broke his left wrist in an army gymnasium during the war, an accident that left his arm two inches shorter than it was before; the technical adjustments this demanded of his batting must have been significant. He was never physically particularly strong and this injury restricted him. His strokes were due to timing rather than power.

There is surely no more arduous task for a Test batsman than opening the innings and Hutton's record shows how equal he was to the challenge: of the 24 batsmen who have scored 5,000 Test runs as openers none averaged more than Hutton's 56.47.

Hutton gave an immense amount to English cricket and when in other circumstances he might have continued for several more years, his race was run within months of him returning home in triumph from Australia in 1955. His back was sore and his mind weary from the fight. The following year he was knighted for services to cricket, only the second professional after Hobbs to be so honoured.

He once very kindly said of me, 'David Gower makes batting look as easy as drinking tea', a lovely compliment, which tempted me to put him even higher in this list of greats!

16. DENNIS LILLEE

Australia 1970–84

In any list of those who were fast bowlers pure and simple, Dennis Lillee must rank very high up. I have placed Malcolm Marshall ahead of him, but there was not that much between them in terms of ability and bowling intelligence. They were both pretty complete packages and both gave me a lot to think about when I faced them. Dennis was very highly regarded among his contemporaries and the likes of Malcolm himself and Imran Khan, among plenty of others, rated him the finest of his generation. He and Andy Roberts both had pace, skill and a great deal of nous, and they set the standard for fast bowling in the mid-1970s. Of the many great quick men who emerged in their wake, most learnt from how those two went about their business.

When Lillee retired from Test cricket in 1984, he had more wickets to his name – 355 at 23.92 – than anyone before him. An important footnote to that is that he also took 67 wickets in 14 World Series 'Supertests', more than any other bowler in that most demanding of environments. World Series was

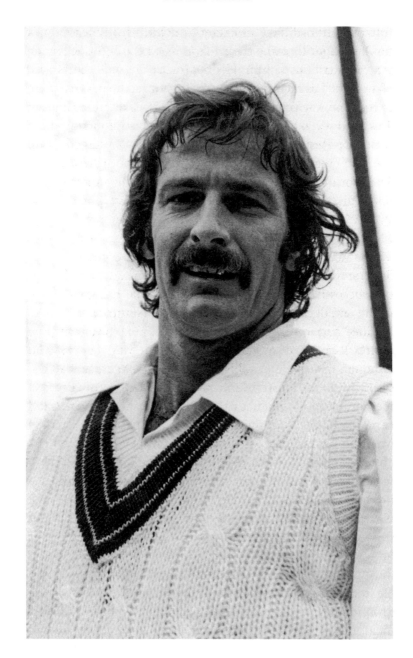

full of extraordinary cricketers, including numerous fast bowlers eager to make their mark, and he still shone, which is a great tribute to him. His nearest rival was Roberts with 50 wickets. His record against Viv Richards, the best batsman of his time, speaks volumes: he took his wicket nine times in Tests and seven times in 'Supertests'. He also stood out in an Australia–Rest of the World series in 1971–72 staged to fill the void created by the cancellation of a South Africa tour. The World team was of high calibre yet Lillee almost single-handedly destroyed them on a typically fast pitch at the WACA with figures of eight for 29. He was the main reason why they were also bowled out cheaply in the first innings of the next game at his beloved Melbourne before Garry Sobers, who by this time had been dismissed by Lillee for two successive ducks, struck back with what has gone down in the annals as one of the great double-centuries.

Lillee had wonderful control and was able to vary his line of attack and pace at will. At his peak he was very fast and although his pace inevitably dipped in later years he had the skill to remain a formidable proposition. One of his most memorable performances that I experienced at first hand came on a pitch of uneven bounce at Melbourne in 1980 when he cut his pace and bowled a mixture of leg- and off-cutters, and took six for 60.

What made Lillee so special was the element of theatre he brought to the occasion. He loved to perform in front of a big crowd, especially at the cavernous MCG where Australian supporters would get behind him and chant his name as he set off on his long, flowing run-up, culminating in the most perfect of actions, a model for any aspiring youngster. He took almost a quarter of all his Test wickets on the ground and bowled his side to some famous victories there, including in the epic Centenary Test of 1977. He possessed tremendous charisma and showmanship, but the desire to play to the gallery and live up to their expectations led him into some ugly incidents which did not reflect particularly well on him – an infamous physical confrontation with Javed Miandad and a notorious attempt to use an aluminium bat high among them.

I have an abiding memory of watching him on television bowling on his first tour of England in 1972, when he took 31 wickets in the series, and he was a captivating sight, with his incredibly long run-up, long hair, and energy. Subsequent to that – and after he had recovered from major back surgery – came the Ashes series in Australia in which he and Jeff Thomson ran amok, highlights of which were also shown on TV at home. I was well aware of the image and reputation long before I ever shared a pitch with him.

That first meeting came in a warm-up match against Western Australia at the WACA on our 1979–80 tour, a few months after Kerry Packer and the cricketing Establishment made their peace and the big stars, of whom he was indisputably one, returned to the fold. It proved a frustrating experience. He bowled me a bouncer which I took right out of the sweet spot of the bat but couldn't quite keep down and satisfaction quickly turned to despair as I saw the ball disappear straight down long leg's throat. Unusually for him, Lillee was not so much triumphant as a little apologetic. Could I claim to have been a little unlucky? Probably not!

We got on well over the years. I think there was some mutual respect. Certainly for my part I held him in huge regard, and I was never going to get involved in a war of words with him. That was not my style. There was a bit of interaction but it was rarely hostile. He liked to snarl and growl at batsmen but sledging depends entirely on whether you think the guy at the other end can play. If you think he's a waste of space, your sledging is going to be contemptuous and heartfelt. If you think he can play a bit, it's much less vitriolic. I sometimes gave cause to irritate him, such as when I played and missed countless times in the early stages of my 98 at Sydney later on during that 1979–80 tour, but on the whole I think we both enjoyed our duels. It was an added challenge to score runs off someone as good as him. You knew if you did you'd played well.

The 1981 series in England was played on some pitches on which the best means of success was for the bowlers to pitch it up and let the ball do the work, and accordingly Lillee, along with Terry Alderman, tailored his methods very well (if not at Headingley where they dropped too short and wide at Ian Botham, with famous consequences). He still had a bit of pace but he was a more mature cricketer and man. When we crossed swords for the last time in Australia in 1982–83 I was in very good form but he got the better of me a couple of times by seaming and swinging the ball back in to me. He was always up to something and you could never afford to relax against him. He described himself as like a bull terrier who would never let go of a batsman once he had him by the throat – and that seems a pretty fair description!

15. BARRY RICHARDS

South Africa 1970

I cannot imagine that anyone who regularly saw Barry Richards play would describe him as anything less than a genius. He could play against the best in all conditions and

there is absolutely no doubt in my mind that he would have had a spectacular Test match career had the opportunity allowed. As it was, opposition to sporting contact with South Africa cut him off at the age of 24 after just one series. As if to show what he might have done, he scored two centuries and more than 500 runs in that one series, which consisted of four matches – all won – against Australia.

Richards was an established and awesome figure in county cricket when I joined Leicestershire in the mid-1970s. He formed one half of a great opening partnership with Gordon Greenidge at Hampshire but there was no doubting which one of them was pre-eminent. People knew what Gordon could do – and he was good enough to finish with more than 100 caps for West Indies and 7,500 Test runs to his name – but there was a feeling that if Barry got in you had more problems.

He had the ultimate gift of making it look an incredibly easy and graceful game. It is the gift of the great: time seems to slow down between the ball leaving the bowler's hand and arriving at the other end. It was as if he was saying to himself, 'Well, let me see now … I think I'll hit this one for four.' It did not matter what length the ball was, he'd score off it. He had a strong bottom hand but he struck the ball majestically through the covers, a position I was expected to patrol when Leicestershire and Hampshire met. It was not a time to let the concentration lapse: you knew that if you dropped BA Richards you could well cost your side the match.

I suspect there's a lasting regret that he didn't get the chance to put some serious figures into the book in official Test cricket. Once it became clear that there was no end in sight to South Africa's isolation, it must have been a hard situation for him to accept. They used to say at Hampshire that it depended what sort of mood he was in as to whether he'd score runs. If there was someone in the crowd he wanted to impress, you'd be guaranteed runs; if there wasn't, maybe not. There was a perceived casual air about him, and this irked some people, but I am in no position to criticise and certainly don't hold it against him that he got bored playing so much county cricket and that he found it hard to maintain the highest standards all the time. It would be hypocritical if I did. He could produce exceptionally special performances when required. He could win matches and entertain as well: substance with very real style.

Even if his critics are right in suggesting that his results could have been yet more exceptional, the figures are still mighty impressive. He scored getting on for 30,000 first-class runs at the exceptionally high average of 54.74, a figure bettered by only five who like him played regular county cricket: Geoff Boycott, Ranjitsinhji, Wally Hammond, Len Hutton and Garry Sobers. In one-day cricket, of which he was an early master, there were more than 8,500 runs at an average of 40.12, which was also high for his era. He scored 80 hundreds in first-class cricket and another 16 in one-dayers. These are hardly the statistics of a wastrel. He helped Hampshire win the county championship in 1973 and the Sunday league in 1975 and 1978 at a time when it was a competition that counted for something. Only rain prevented them retaining the championship in 1974, a year in which he scored 225 not out in a match at Trent Bridge in which only two other players passed 30. He helped Natal win four Currie Cups outright and powered South Australia to the Sheffield Shield title during a legendary season with them in 1970–71 in which he averaged 109.85. He plundered 356 off Western Australia in Perth – 325 of them on the first day alone – and 224 and 146 in two games against Ray Illingworth's MCC touring side, a team that regained the Ashes for England. On a dollar a run for the season, he scored 1,538 in ten matches!

A measure of his innate quality is that in his very first season in county cricket in 1968, and having played relatively little in English conditions before, Richards scored 2,395 first-class runs, more than anyone else in a wet summer, and finished second in the averages only to Boycott.

For all those South African guys who couldn't play Test cricket, the ultimate challenge was World Series and Barry was very good at World Series. I remember going to watch him bat for the World XI on the trotting track at Gloucester Park when I spent a winter in grade cricket in Perth and he sent the ball disappearing to all parts against an Australia attack spearheaded by Dennis Lillee. He scored 207 out of a first-day score of 433 for one. World Series was mighty tough cricket not always played on good pitches (even if the Gloucester Park one looked pretty flat!) with, and against, a spectacularly good collection of cricketers being made to work hard for their money. It was a very good product and better than Test cricket at the time. In five World Series 'Supertests' he scored 554 runs, averaging 79.14.

Mike Procter, who grew up playing alongside and against Richards (they spent a season together in Gloucestershire's second team in 1965), said that he knew of no weakness in his game and that he would certainly have nominated him as the batsman to play for his life. When Jeff Thomson was at the height of his powers, Richards scored 96 and 69 against him for Hampshire against the touring Australians in 1975 (although it is true he had to retire in his second innings after being hit in the groin by Thommo!). Even in his late 30s, he was good enough to deal effectively with the decidedly hostile fast bowling of Sylvester Clarke when a rebel West Indian side toured South Africa. Lillee thought him the 'personification of batting perfection'. So do I.

14. JACQUES KALLIS

South Africa 1995–2013

The year-round demands of the modern game count against genuine all-rounders sustaining a career in Test match cricket. Andrew Flintoff was influential for England with both bat and ball for a few years before his body complained but Jacques Kallis confounded the argument that it could not be done for a prolonged period. His fast-medium bowling may have been his second string but from 1998 to 2008 he averaged 22 wickets a year in Tests as well as 875 runs. He was the nearest thing Test cricket had seen to a great all-rounder since the days of Imran Khan and Ian Botham in the early 1980s. He was also a superb slip catcher, in the same class as Botham himself.

Kallis was central to the success the South Africa team built over the years. He was the rock on which a powerful batting unit was built, lent invaluable support to a strong pace attack with the ball, swinging it markedly when conditions were right, and missed very few of the many edges that came his way in the cordon. In late 2008, South Africa became the first visiting team for 15 years to win a series in Australia – Kallis contributing 187 runs and seven wickets – and a few months later they ended Australia's long reign at number 1 in the Test rankings. They only stayed top for a few months but regained the position in England in 2012, when Kallis had an outstanding match at The Oval, scoring an unbeaten 182 and reviving his bowling to good effect, his first-innings dismissals of Kevin Pietersen and Ian Bell shifting the game's momentum. South Africa were still number 1 when he played the last of his 166 Tests the following year.

Kallis's Test figures are truly awesome – 13,289 runs, 292 wickets and 200 catches – but he was generally not a player to turn a game with an explosive passage of play in the way Imran or Botham might have done. That was not his style and nor was it South Africa's. His sheer dependability suited a team that tended to put a premium on minimising risks.

Rather like Sachin Tendulkar, who alone has bettered his tally of 45 Test centuries, Kallis had an immaculate technique and an amazing ability to stay focused on the business of scoring runs, whatever the potential distractions. Some observers felt he was impervious to the match situation and simply played for himself, but this was not a view shared by his teammates, who insisted there was no more selfless cricketer. Perhaps he was simply concentrating so thoroughly that he appeared to be disregarding everything that did not affect the next delivery. There were no fundamental flaws in his method, especially as he was happy to play within himself for the most part. In fact, if he had a fault this might have been it: his tempo was the same whether he was facing the bowling of Bangladesh or Australia. But there was no arguing with the results: Kallis's Test average of 55.37 is higher than Tendulkar's, and indeed higher than every other batsmen with 8,000 runs to their name, with the exception of Garry Sobers and Kumar Sangakkara.

It is hard to recall times when he appeared ruffled, save for a fiery spell from Flintoff at Edgbaston in 2008 which ended with Kallis's off stump being sent flying several yards by a ball that swung late. In Kallis's defence, he and several of his teammates had problems picking up the ball from Flintoff against the backdrop of the committee room windows above a sightscreen not tall enough to do its job. He was also kept relatively quiet by Muttiah Muralitharan and did not score a Test century against Sri Lanka until after Murali had retired, but he was hardly alone in that.

Kallis, a protégé of Duncan Fletcher at Western Province, did not take long to make his mark after being first chosen for South Africa at the age of 20. He struck a stylish half-century in his fifth one-day international against England in Durban and in his seventh Test match scored a match-saving hundred in one of the toughest of all environments, versus Australia in Melbourne, against an attack that included Glenn McGrath and Shane Warne. That performance came after some low scores in his early games and after his part in a tour of Pakistan had been cut short by appendicitis, but there were to be few more hiccups after that. A season at Middlesex played an important part in his development. I remember John Hardy, who played at Western Province and was a mate of Jacques', saying when he was on the way up that he would be a stupendous player, and so it proved.

Kallis quickly became an automatic selection and the only time when his methods were questioned by the South Africans themselves was in 2007 when some slow scores at the World Cup led to him being left out of the squad for the inaugural World Twenty20. But he learnt his lesson quickly and was the second highest run-scorer in his second season at the Indian Premier League.

Kallis's Test record against Australia was one of the best measures of his quality. He scored more than 2,000 Test runs against them at an average of 45.43 with five hundreds, one of only six batsmen to score 2,000 runs against them since 1995 (he also took 51 wickets). If it was a long time before South Africa had the satisfaction of winning a series against them, they did get there in the end, beating them in

Australia in 2012–13 (when Kallis scored 147 in Brisbane) as well as 2008–09.

Valuable though his bowling was, Kallis was probably underrated as a bowler, partly because the batting naturally took priority and partly because he himself was sometimes reluctant to bowl. You could understand why, because massive run-making takes time and effort, but he was good enough and strong enough to be a frontline bowler alone. He could bowl a really heavy ball, was deceptively quick and very tidy. He once bowled South Africa to victory in a Test match at Headingley with figures of six for 54 that anyone would be proud of.

What was astonishing was that he was so durable for so long. He had to look after himself in the end, which was why he cut back on his bowling, but by then he had got through an immense amount of work. Quite apart from what he did in Tests, he scored 11,579 runs and took 273 wickets in one-day internationals.

13. SYDNEY BARNES

England 1901–14

Sydney Barnes was by common consent the greatest bowler to appear before the First World War. Many good judges long after that still maintained there had never been better, and it is not hard to see why. Barnes's record is astonishing. He also won his reputation despite being a cussed so-and-so who made it hard for people to like him. Maybe they didn't much like him but they certainly admired and respected him.

Not that being contrary and cussed are rare traits among great bowlers; it is by nurturing an inner flame of hostility that some of them are capable of rising to such heights. But Barnes really didn't like batsmen, and he especially didn't like those administrators and captains who expected him to kowtow to them. If he'd liked administrators more he would certainly have played more Test matches and finished with an even better record than he did. Asked the best captain he played under, he said, 'Me. When I have been bowling, I have been captain.'

Perhaps the surprise was that Barnes played as many Test matches as he did – 27 of them across 13 years – because he took part in very little county championship cricket, preferring to take his services to the leagues where the money was better and the demands less onerous, and to turn out for Staffordshire in the Minor Counties championship. This set him at odds with the committee at Lancashire and made it easier for England captains and selectors to overlook his qualities. Having been picked on a hunch by Archie MacLaren for a tour of Australia in 1901–02 and done well before breaking down injured, Barnes was chosen for only one home Test in the next six years. The penny finally dropped after he returned to Australia in 1907–08 and proved himself, in the eyes of the Australians at least, the best bowler in the world. Thereafter he became a near-regular in the England side up to the outbreak of war in 1914 and might have continued Test cricket afterwards had he not declined to go back to Australia once more in 1920–21 – at the age of 47 – because the MCC refused to allow his wife to join him (a privilege they extended to the captain Johnny Douglas).

His finest hour was probably the 1911–12 tour of Australia when he and Frank Foster, the young Warwickshire all-rounder, spearheaded England to a 4–1 series triumph. Barnes produced one of the great spells of Test match bowling on a perfect pitch on the first morning of the second Test at Melbourne, when he bowled a spell of nine overs, including six maidens and taking four wickets for just three runs. This exemplified his ability to tame the best batsmen in even the most favourable batting conditions; his victims were Warren Bardsley, Clem Hill, Charles Kelleway and Warwick Armstrong. He dismissed Hill and Victor Trumper, the two finest Australian batsmen of the time, 13 times and 11 times respectively, and Herbie Taylor, the leading South African, eight times. Only ten individual hundreds were scored against England in the 27 Tests Barnes played.

Not the least of his strengths was an amazing stamina that allowed him to bowl for hours on end if need be, as was often the case in Australia where pitches offered little help and Barnes, who could bowl as well with new or old ball, was consistently the most likely wicket-taker. During that 1911–12 tour, he got through an astonishing 297 overs in the five Tests, taking 34 wickets, which remains the second best haul by an England bowler in Australia. In the second Test of the 1901–02 tour he bowled 80.1 overs, a workload that probably contributed to the injury that prevented him bowling in much of the next game. Setting aside that game and a rain-ruined contest in 1912, Barnes averaged 313 balls per match in the other 25 Tests he took part in, which is the kind of burden even most spinners would baulk at (Muttiah Muralitharan averaged more balls than this, but not Shane Warne).

It was not just throughout whole matches and whole tours that he remained durable; his career was immense in its length. He played professionally from the age of 21 until he was 67 and during that time showed few signs

of deterioration: in all competitive matches, he took a staggering 6,229 wickets at an average of just 8.33. In 1928, when he was 55 years old, he played for Wales against the touring West Indians and returned match figures of 12 for 118 (they said he was the best bowler they faced all tour). A month later, he faced his former county Lancashire, who were in their third straight year as champions, and took eight for 87 from 49 overs. The following year, representing Minor Counties against the South Africans, his first-innings analysis was 32-11-41-8.

Standing 6ft 1in, Barnes bowled brisk medium-pace with a high action. He was immensely accurate and could cut and swing the ball both ways, although his stock delivery was delivered wide of the crease and broke back from leg. If he got the ball to swerve through the air before pitching – as he often did – he became virtually unplayable. The key was how sharply he could spin the ball with his big fingers. 'I spun the skin off my fingers,' he once said. 'I bowled with blood smearing the ball.' As for his tactics, his assessment was this: 'I never bowled at the wickets: I bowled at the stroke. I intended the batsman to make a stroke, then I tried to beat it.'

Even though his Test career was not long even by the standards of the day, Barnes's haul of 189 wickets was easily the best of the pre-First World War period and in fact remained the world Test record until 1935 when it was overtaken by Australia's Clarrie Grimmett. Although conditions favoured bowlers more during his England career than they did later, his statistics were impressive in many ways. Of the top 20 wicket-takers of the pre-1914 era, for example, only George Lohmann (with 112 wickets at 10.75) had a better average than Barnes, and Lohmann's figures were boosted by some easy pickings against South Africa in matches that were not at the time even regarded as official Tests. Barnes's average of 16.43 and strike rate of 41.65 are both unmatched by any post-1900 bowler with 100 Test wickets.

What turned out to be his final Test series was statistically the most extraordinary. Touring South Africa in 1913–14 for a series played on coir matting pitches, as was then common in South Africa, Barnes claimed a match haul of 17 for 159 in the second Test in Johannesburg and 49 wickets in the series. The 17-wicket haul remained the best in any Test match until beaten by Jim Laker's famous 19 for 90 against Australia at Old Trafford in 1956, while no one has ever matched 49 wickets in a series. Amazingly, Barnes only took part in four of the five matches: in characteristic fashion, he refused to play in the final contest after the local authorities (in his view) reneged on an agreement to have a collection for him.

12. IAN BOTHAM

England 1978–92

Ian Botham, whom I played alongside in 87 Test matches, was a genius of self-belief. He never knowingly admitted to self-doubt and although there must have been times, especially against the mighty West Indies, when even he surely privately wondered whether the Botham magic could be made to work, this outward expression of supreme confidence in his own ability – backed up by immense talent – served him spectacularly well. However tough the job, he believed he could find a way to get it done, and more often than not he did, carrying the rest of the team along with him. Such players are few and far between – Shane Warne was a later example for Australia – and accordingly a captain's dream. For the period that he was in his pomp, from 1977 to 1981 with the ball, and from 1981 to 1985 with the bat, Ian's self-belief was England's 12th man.

He was not someone who saved performances for games that did not matter. He produced many of his greatest efforts against Australia: in 36 matches against them, he scored 1,673 runs, took 148 wickets and held 57 catches. Few Test all-rounders have ever been as effective as he was with bat and ball at the same time: five times he scored a century and took a five-for in the same Test match, a feat no one else has achieved more than twice. He was spectacular to watch and exhilarating to be anywhere near.

Sometimes, of course, the refusal to countenance failure – inculcated by his mentor Brian Close – took him beyond what was possible and he needed reining in, but most of the time it was hard not to think that England's best plan was to go with our talisman. When I was appointed England captain for a second time in 1989 I brought him back into the side despite the fact that following injury he had recently not played much cricket because even then – and Ian was by now 33 years of age – I still had absolute belief in him and he still had absolute belief in himself. As it happened, it did not work out for him that summer but then it did not work out for any of us as we were trounced by Allan Border's rejuvenated Australians.

Ian instinctively knew how to win games of cricket, which is a knack that not even some very good players master. Yet it is one he had from the outset, as he showed in one of his very early games for Somerset when as an 18-year-old he was hit by an Andy Roberts bouncer, spat out a couple of broken teeth, and carried on to see his county home in a Benson & Hedges Cup quarter-final against Hampshire. And it was this same knack, of course, that was at the heart of his heroics in the incredible Ashes series of 1981 – three Test matches in a row won and three man-of-the-match awards in a row for Ian. In each game – first at Headingley, then Edgbaston and Old Trafford – his telling contributions came in the second innings when the fate of the contest remained in the balance, or, as was the case at Headingley, ridiculously in Australia's favour. England's hopes were pretty slim too at Edgbaston, where curiously he actually needed some persuading to bowl again with Australia closing in on their target: once he got the ball in his hand he was irresistible, though, and finished the game with a spell of five wickets in 28 balls.

Other less celebrated interventions at the business end of games came at The Oval in 1979, when India were racing towards what would have been a record-breaking run-chase of 438 before Ian applied the brakes with a catch, three wickets and a run-out to earn England a draw, and at Melbourne in 1982 when he finally broke (courtesy of a juggled catch between slips Chris Tavare and Geoff Miller) a stubborn last-wicket partnership between Border and Jeff Thomson to give England an agonising three-run win. No wonder we questioned who wrote his scripts.

Not that every game Ian won went to the wire. He orchestrated quite a few routs as well, perhaps the most astonishing of which came in the Golden Jubilee Test in Mumbai in 1980 where he scored a century and took 13 wickets as the ball seamed markedly on a pitch that would have been more at home in England than India. The conditions, though, were hot and humid and bowling fast would have been very hard work for anyone lacking Ian's iron strength. He thought nothing of it and on one day

bowled 24 overs unchanged. In the interests of historical accuracy it ought to be pointed out that during that game he was not necessarily burdened by a full night's sleep. Off the field as on it, Ian was one of the most full-on men you'll ever meet, something I, along with countless teammates and opponents, learnt to our cost!

When he was at his best, before his back started giving him trouble, he was the most dangerous swing bowler in the world. He was tall, lithe and strong, and always willing, and had been well schooled in the art by Tom Cartwright at Somerset. When I first played alongside him for England in 1978, I saw batsmen who did not know which way the ball was going to swing: they either missed it or nicked it. There was some criticism that he was often playing against teams weakened by defections to World Series but the way he bowled then he would have got out even the best. The figures did not lie. In just four years he had taken 200 Test wickets in just 41 matches (only four bowlers have ever got to this landmark in fewer games). If he was less consistently menacing thereafter, he still had his moments. In 1985, I used him in short bursts as a strike bowler against Australia and he was mighty effective; our mistake was to try the same ploy in the West Indies a few months later. Nor was he ever too proud to get a wicket with a bad ball: again like Warne, he would do what was necessary to make a breakthrough. I once saw him take a five-for in a Test match in Melbourne (in 1986–87) when only two-thirds fit, bowling all manner of filth, and you walked off the field thinking, 'How on earth did he manage that?'

He was by then the leading wicket-taker in Test history, a position he held for two years. It says something about Ian that none of the other holders of this record were anything like as influential with the bat or came close to rivalling his

14 Test match hundreds. As a batsman, Ian was at his best as a counter-attacker, but his play was usually fundamentally sound, based on a good technique, nice balance and a high backlift. He was sometimes portrayed as something of a village blacksmith with a bat in his hand but there was far more to him than that. To ping the ball to all parts of Brisbane against Merv Hughes, with nothing more than a floppy white hat for head protection, as he did while scoring a century there in 1986, demonstrated that.

He was also one of the best fielders you could hope to see. He was good in any position but absolutely brilliant in the slips. It was quite unnerving standing alongside him in the slips – he would be at second, me at third – because he stood much closer to the bat than was normal as he hated to see the ball dropping short and he reckoned that even with less time to react he could hold on to the chances that came his way (there was that self-belief again). Because of his advanced position we then adopted a 'W' formation, with him ahead of both first and third slips. If I or anyone else at third had been in front of him we would have been almost alongside the batsman!

The flaws in Ian's career have been well chronicled. He was unlucky during his brief spell as England captain to come up against West Indies at a time when they were pre-eminent, but his leadership style was not in any case to everyone's liking. He wasn't all things to all men. His record against West Indies was modest, even allowing for their undeniable strength. There were the off-field controversies too. There was the admission of drug-taking and the consequent ban, and a number of scrapes splashed across tabloid newspapers. His might not have been the life of an angel; nor was he the ultimate role model. But by God you would gamble on having him in your side.

11. IMRAN KHAN

Pakistan 1971–92

Imran Khan is indisputably Pakistan's greatest cricketer. As an all-rounder he bears comparison with the best there have ever been, a skilful fast bowler and resourceful batsman with a solid defence; but it is as a leader that he really stood out. History shows that Pakistan are a notoriously difficult team to captain but he had the charisma and stature to unify them and drive them to play above themselves, and that is quite a talent.

His finest hour was undoubtedly guiding Pakistan to their first World Cup triumph in 1992, top-scoring with 72 in the final against England after famously imploring his team earlier in the tournament when their hopes hung by a thread to fight 'like cornered tigers'. But he has to his name a number of other outstanding achievements. He led Pakistan to their first Test series wins in both India – obviously a huge thing in his country – and England, and he also led Pakistan to three drawn series in a row against West Indies when West Indies were at the height of their powers.

Pakistan in fact were the first side to seriously challenge West Indian supremacy. When they won in Guyana in 1988 it was the first time in ten years that West Indies had lost a home Test; Imran took 11 wickets in the game. In his career as a whole, Imran claimed 80 wickets at 21.18 apiece against West Indies, an incredible record given how strong they were at the time. He scored some important runs against them too, notably in his final series against them in 1990–91 when

he averaged 50.33 (his overall average against West Indies was 27.67).

Imran, who led Pakistan on and off for ten years from 1982 to 1992, mentored some fine players during that period, notably fast bowlers Wasim Akram and Waqar Younis, who swung the ball at pace even greater distances than he did. Imran had the bearing of a leader and for the most part the players followed. Captaincy elevated his game to a striking degree, averaging 50.55 with the bat and 19.90 with the ball.

He turned himself into a considerable bowler with an astonishing record inside Pakistan where visiting fast bowlers tended to find life desperately hard. Imran himself took 163 wickets at 19.20 apiece there, a better record than he had elsewhere (his overall record was a hugely impressive 362 wickets in 88 Tests at 22.81 each; no one had taken more for Pakistan at the time he retired). I never faced him in Pakistan as he was nursing a stress fracture that prevented him from bowling for the best part of two years when I toured there in 1983–84, but I encountered him in England in 1982 and 1987 and he was a major force both times. In three Tests in 1982, when we were perhaps a little fortunate to win the series 2–1, he scored 212 runs and took 21 wickets; in 1987, he again took 21 wickets and was the match-winner with the ball in the one game that had a positive outcome at Headingley, bowling immaculately to take seven for 40 in the second innings. I was one of his victims but at least had the small satisfaction of scoring 50.

Imran, who was at Oxford in the early 1970s and from there joined Worcestershire, started out as a brisk medium-pacer but through determination and intelligence turned himself into a genuine fast bowler of quality. I remember facing him in one of my earliest games for Leicestershire at around the time he was stepping up his pace. It was the day after I took an early exit from university and we were playing a Benson & Hedges Cup quarter-final at Worcester on a good old New Road pitch with pace and bounce. I was caught at slip off him and the ball carried a long way behind me, always a good measure of someone's speed. In county cricket in the period from the mid-1970s to mid-1980s, Imran would have been up there with Mike Procter and Malcolm Marshall as among the best at swinging the ball at pace.

Perhaps the thing that completed his education was joining World Series, from which he emerged a far better bowler, learning from watching and working with so many other fine fast bowlers recruited by Kerry Packer. In the years he played from 1980 to 1986, either side of his lay-off for the stress fracture, he was taking his Test wickets at very cheap cost. In 1982 he returned what remain the best match figures for Pakistan in Tests of 14 for 114 against Sri Lanka in Lahore. The following winter he took an incredible 40 wickets at 13.95 in six Tests against India.

What the Pakistan bowlers, led by Imran and Sarfraz Nawaz, seemed to understand better than everyone else was the mysterious art of swinging the old ball, and for a batsman, coping with anyone who could move the ball – whether old or new – both ways was always a challenge. You worked hard to get your runs.

The early 1980s was a great era for all-rounders with Imran, Botham, Richard Hadlee and Kapil Dev all doing great things and rivalling each other for the status of top dog. In terms of bowling, Imran was perhaps consistently the quickest of them. Botham had times where he bowled with the same sort of pace, Hadlee could bowl a sharp delivery if needed but in comparison was slightly down on pace overall, and Kapil was more brisk medium than brisk. But they all moved the ball in the air or hit the seam, or both, and that was really what made them so difficult to face. Statistically, Imran and Hadlee stood well out in front, averaging around 22 while Botham and Kapil took their wickets at a cost in the high 20s, a reflection really that they were unable to maintain their early brilliance into older age.

Botham probably ranked first as a batsman but Imran, who began his career down the order, developed into a seriously good top-order player and accordingly ended up with six Test hundreds to his name (Botham made 14, Kapil eight and Hadlee two). Imran kept on improving and became a class batsman in all forms. Indeed, towards the end of his career he was playing more as a batsman who bowled than a bowler who batted, and when he scored those runs in the 1992 World Cup final he was batting at number 3. His Test record with the bat was highly respectable, an average of 37.69 comparing well to Botham's 33.54, Kapil's 31.05 and Hadlee's 27.16. What gives Imran pre-eminence in this all-rounder fest is his stature as a leader of a national side that had previously lacked any direction.

Since Imran, Pakistan cricket has rarely been stable. Talented players continue to be produced in extraordinary numbers given the absence of a coherent domestic structure but it has been engulfed in more than one corruption scandal, while a terrorist attack on a touring Sri Lanka team in 2009 has forced them since to set up a new home in the Middle East. Imran himself has entered politics in the ambitious hope of addressing his country's many problems.

10. WG GRACE

England 1880–99

Ah, yes, good old WG. The famous doctor has become something of a target for mockery – famous for his beard, his size (he was struggling to bend to field the ball by the time of his last Test match), his gamesmanship and his shamateurism – but his achievements really were things of stupendous substance. His legend would not have endured 100 years after his death if they were not. His name still resonates with the wider public, even though they may know little about the sport he did more than anyone else to popularise.

In the way that great men do, Grace came along at just the right time to capitalise on an evolutionary turning point in the game. By 1864, when Grace turned 16, overarm bowling had been legalised, a decision that rapidly turned cricket into something that the modern generation might relate to, while an annual county championship was rapidly taking shape. Grace proved so successful that people turned up in their thousands to watch him play, not only in England but when he toured Australia with English sides in 1873–74 and 1891–92. No cricketer during his lifetime had such an effect on gates, so it is hardly surprising that – amateur or not – he demanded large slices of the financial pie (his fee for the 1873–74 tour was ten times that offered the professionals).

Cricket may have still been in a developmental stage, but young WG did not lack for help in honing his astonishing skills. The eighth of nine children to cricket-loving parents in Downend, Bristol, he grew up in the slipstream of an elder brother, Edward Mills Grace, who might have been remembered as the finest all-rounder of his day had not young William Gilbert been so diligent in learning from him all that he could. They did much to make Gloucestershire the dominant county during the mid-1870s and make the Gentlemen (amateurs) competitive in their matches with the Players (professionals).

Had WG not risen to the top so phenomenally fast, there might have been more chance of someone questioning whether he should actually have been playing on the amateur side. He scored his first double century (for an England XI against Surrey in 1866) at the age of 18, at a time when scores of such size were extremely rare. Four years later, he was generally accepted as the best cricketer there had ever been. A few years after that, he was simply referred to as 'The Champion'. No wonder. He routinely dominated the national batting averages by a distance: from 1869 to 1880 he was top in all but two years and generally averaged more than 50 when few could manage to top 30. In the 1871 season, he scored 2,739 runs (average 78.25), a tally that was not beaten for a quarter of a century.

With football lagging behind cricket in its development, WG was the major sporting personality of his time and as recognisable as Queen Victoria. On the Grace Gates at Lord's, which were erected in 1923, eight years after his death and with Bradman still some way short of making his first-class debut, he was described succinctly as 'The Great Cricketer'.

There were several secrets to his success. Standing 6ft and powerfully built, he developed a technique that could destroy even the best fast bowling on pitches that were often dangerously rough. He also opened up the leg side as a scoring area when many considered it a style malfunction to

do anything but hit the ball straight back to where it came from or through the covers. Thanks to a good method, a lot of patience and total dedication to the task, he showed just how long it was possible to bat. In the space of eight days in 1876, he scored 344 against Kent (the highest first-class score then recorded), 177 against Nottinghamshire and 318 against Yorkshire. No cricketer had ever been so scientific.

There was a lot more to him than his batting, though. For many years he was also among the most effective bowlers in the country, bowling brisk round-arm medium-pace then slow flighted off-breaks, off which he fielded superbly. He took 100 wickets in a season nine times between 1874 and 1886 and performed the match double of 100 runs and 10 wickets a total of 17 times in his career; no one else apart from George Giffen of Australia has ever done so more than six times.

He was so much better than his peers that he might easily have got bored with the lack of competition. Indeed, in 1873 the *Sporting Gazette* complained that he was ruining cricket and asked, 'What is to be done with him?' Fortunately for him, Test cricket came along and the regular exchange of tours between England and Australia presented him with fresh challenges.

Grace scored England's first-ever Test century in the first Test ever staged on English soil at The Oval in 1880 in a match in which his elder brother Edward and their ill-fated younger brother Fred, who was to die within weeks, also played. He soon became England's captain of choice right through to 1899 when, at the age of 50, he finally accepted that time had caught up with him. Not that he gave up cricket altogether: he played on in first-class cricket until 1908 and his 60th year.

As with Tendulkar, longevity was one of the most impressive things about Grace. His first-class career spanned more than

40 years; he scored 54,896 runs, took 2,876 wickets and held 887 catches (as well as executing five stumpings in occasional appearances as a wicketkeeper). Only four batsmen have ever scored more runs, only five bowlers have ever taken more wickets, only one non-wicketkeeper (Frank Woolley) has held more catches.

Although inevitably his form declined in his later years, he enjoyed a famous Indian summer in 1895 when he turned 47, scoring 1,000 runs before the end of May (a feat never achieved before) and recording his hundredth hundred at a time when no one else had managed more than 41.

There is no shortage of stories about WG's sharp practice – of him putting the bails back in the groove and claiming that the wind had blown them off, and of him rounding on opponents in mid-appeal and announcing, 'The public have come to watch me bat, not you bowl.' How true they are, who knows. But there were also plenty willing to testify to his decency. Lord Harris, another England captain of the time, called him 'the kindest and most sympathetic cricketer I have ever played with'.

9. MALCOLM MARSHALL

West Indies 1978–91

One of the trickiest questions is who the best bowler was I ever faced. Inevitably my mind turns to the West Indies quick men who gave me the most torrid times of my career. Trying to pick one out, given all their strengths and differences, is not easy but the palm would have to go to

Malcolm Marshall. I was far from the only batsman of my generation who felt like that. And perhaps most persuasively of all, his West Indian peers rated him ever so highly. Andy Roberts and Michael Holding both conceded that he was probably the best. My respect and admiration for him was one of the reasons why in 1990 I joined Hampshire, where he had long been an established star – respect, admiration and an instinct for preservation that saw this as a sure-fire way to reduce the chances of me having to face his bowling.

'Macko' had blistering pace when he wanted it, and could pepper you with bouncers when he felt like it, but he also possessed the nous to temper that pace when conditions suggested he would fare better by slowing down, pitching the ball up and swinging it late both ways. Everything about him was quick, from the sprinting run-up to the quick action, to the ball that whistled around your ears. His instinct for assessing conditions was only matched by his knack for working out what tactics, and what field settings, worked best for each opponent. He knew his mind and knew what he was trying to do. He was among the sharpest of competitors.

Roberts was credited with, pardon the pun, marshalling the long line of great Caribbean fast bowlers of the 1970s and 1980s but Marshall took things to a new level of sophistication. They know about fast bowling in Bridgetown and I remember once watching him from the stands there playing for Barbados in an island game: he was moving the ball around to the alarm of the batsmen in an exhibition that had the small gathering of locals looking on with me purring their approval of a master technician at work.

What made him stand out? I reckon he was my equivalent of the previous generation facing Jeff Thomson in his pomp. 'Thommo' may have had a couple of miles an hour on Marshall but at the speeds at which they were operating that did not make a lot of difference. The great thing about Thommo was that he would keep coming at you all day long, and he would keep getting bounce. Marshall was the same: always coming. He had a lovely fluid action that disguised quite how much effort he was putting in and it was amazing that he never seemed to get tired. You needed to be aware of that extra effort. He wouldn't necessarily bowl at the speed of light all the day but he could step things up at any moment if he wanted to. I remember at Antigua in '86, when England were battling to avoid yet another defeat at West Indian hands, I'd managed to bat a long time for 90 when out of nowhere on a docile pitch Marshall managed to bowl me a snorter of a bouncer – one of those balls that 'got big'. In truth I would contest the validity of the dismissal (honest!) as I was given out caught behind even though the ball narrowly missed my glove before flicking my shoulder, but it was the fact that Marshall had suddenly extracted so much extra bounce that produced the wicket.

Marshall was relatively small for a fast bowler at 5ft 11in and this made him particularly awkward. The Marshall bouncer tended to skid on to you. If a taller man dropped the ball short, there was a fair chance it would go over your head. But his best bouncers gave you nowhere to go and nowhere to hide. A lot of people besides Mike Gatting, who once famously and painfully misjudged a hook shot against Marshall, found this out to their cost. He broke my right wrist on that 1986 tour, although I didn't realise it was actually broken until about a year later when an X-ray on another blow, this time from Merv Hughes, highlighted the damage. I just thought it hurt, a lot.

I first came across him on a Young England tour of West Indies in 1976 and even though he was only 18 years old it was pretty clear that he was someone I might be coming

up against a lot more in the future. In fact, because of the emergence of World Series, he was chosen to tour with West Indies just two years later after only one first-class appearance for Barbados. He had to wait a few years to become a regular in the Test side but his early promotion meant that he was able to learn on the job from some of the finest of fast bowling minds. He also learnt a lot from joining Hampshire as a replacement overseas player for Roberts. His breakthrough year was 1983, when he took 21 wickets in a home Test series against India before hot-footing to England to take 134 wickets in the championship for Hampshire (it is now almost 50 years since anyone took more wickets in an English season – Derek Underwood with 136 in 1967 the last to have done so). Shortly after, he took 33 wickets in six Tests in what are usually arduous fast bowling conditions in India, having been given the new ball for West Indies for the first time on the suggestion of Holding.

It was a role he relished and after that he just got better and better. Even though he was playing in a mighty powerful attack, he regularly proved himself the dominant fast bowler on either side, never more so than during the 1988 series in England when he took 35 wickets in the five matches at just 12.65 apiece. West Indies never lost a Test series in which he featured and by the time of his last Test in 1991 he stood as the leading wicket-taker in West Indies history to that point (376 in 81 matches), with an average of 20.94 unmatched by any out-and-out fast bowler of the 20th century.

Marshall, raised by his mother and grandparents after his father died when he was an infant, grew up idolising Garry Sobers but his dreams of becoming a fully fledged all-rounder never quite materialised, even if he was a more than useful lower-order batsman (he scored seven first-class hundreds but his Test best was 92). He was a great cricketer but also a lovely man who gave his all for the teams he played for. He was mortified at missing out on Hampshire's cup final wins of 1988 and 1991, especially as he had also tasted defeat by one run in the NatWest Trophy in 1990, but this made victory all the sweeter when it came in the Benson & Hedges Cup in 1992. There was never any element of him keeping things to himself; on the contrary he enjoyed sharing information and this made him a wonderful coach in his later years, notably at Natal where he mentored Shaun Pollock among others. His early death from cancer in 1999 at the age of 41 was a desperate loss to all his many friends in the game and beyond.

8. WALLY HAMMOND

England 1927–47

Wally Hammond was a giant among England cricketers and their premier batsman in the period between Jack Hobbs and Len Hutton while offering them so much more besides. He was a superb slip catcher and a highly able fast-medium bowler who fared best in Tests on the harder overseas pitches. Tall and strong, he was capable of taking great workloads in his stride and was rarely out of the action for long. There were similarities in style with Jacques Kallis as a Test all-rounder: both were bowlers who could have accomplished more if their batting had not taken priority, and both were natural fielders, but wonderful technician though Kallis was, Hammond was certainly the more imperious, attacking and influential batsman. England never lost when Hammond

scored a hundred, as he did on 22 occasions – a national record until Alastair Cook overhauled him in 2012. He also lost only one of six series as England captain after giving up his professional status to take on the job.

Hammond was not lucky though. The only son of a Royal Artillery major who was killed in the First World War, his career stalled for two years over a battle for his services between Kent, the county of his birth, and Gloucestershire, the county he ended up serving for 20 seasons. Serious illness cost him a season at a crucial stage in his development and then when he did establish himself as the world's best batsman, along came a diminutive Australian called Don Bradman to steal the position from him. When he led England on a tour of Australia after the Second World War, the team were not ready to resume serious Test cricket and he himself was 43 years old and not fully fit; unsurprisingly his team took a hammering and he bowed out from international cricket a loser. In retirement in South Africa, he lost most of his money in bad investments, and spent his final years struggling with ill-health following a car accident before dying in Natal in 1965, aged 62.

He had a reputation, too, as a somewhat moody and uncommunicative person, which was sadly at odds with the cricket he played because teammates, opponents and those watching from the stands all testified to the glory of Hammond in full flow. 'He was a batsman of the classical, majestic school,' Bradman said. 'Of lovely athletic build, light as a ballet dancer on his feet, always beautifully balanced ...' Bert Oldfield, who stood behind the stumps for many of Hammond's great innings against Australia, described him as 'the perfect batting artist'. Tom Goddard, a Gloucestershire and England teammate, reckoned he was even better than Bradman.

Bradman said he never saw anyone so strong on the off-side as Hammond and it was for his cover-driving that Hammond was best remembered. There is a celebrated photograph of him cover-driving, his trademark handkerchief hanging out of his right pocket. In his early years he was a particularly aggressive and adventurous batsman before England's demands meant that he had to rein himself in and grind out the really big scores then needed to win Test matches in Australia, where games were played to a finish. On the 1928–29 tour, which England won 4–1, Hammond contributed a then-record 905 runs. He batted seven and a half hours for 251 in Sydney, another six and three-quarter hours for 200 in Melbourne, and then spent a total of almost 12 hours at the crease in Adelaide while scoring 119 in the first innings and 177 in the second.

Hammond's appetite for runs was immense – what you might call Bradmanesque if it were not a phrase that would have annoyed him. He scored seven double-centuries in Tests (only Bradman with 12, Kumar Sangakkara with 11, and Brian Lara with nine have made more) and no one has scored more doubles against Australia (Hammond made four to Lara's three, while Graeme Pollock, VVS Laxman and Sachin Tendulkar scored two apiece). In all first-class cricket, Hammond's 36 scores of 200 or more has only been beaten by Bradman (37). His 336 not out against New Zealand at Auckland in 1933 was briefly the world Test record score before being beaten by Len Hutton's 364 in 1938 and while the bowling may not have been the strongest he made his runs at a tremendous rate, his whole innings occupying less than five and a half hours. In all Tests, spanning 85 matches from 1927 to 1947, he scored 7,249 at an average of 58.45. He held the Test run-scoring record from 1937 until 1970 and of the 39 batsmen who, as of 1 January 2015, have scored more

Test runs, only Sangakkara has done so at a higher average.

These are seriously impressive figures but he did experience some difficult times against Australia, notably in England in 1930 and 1934 when he ended up dropping down the order from his favoured number 3 position in the hope of rediscovering form. Australia during his time possessed two great leg-spin and googly bowlers in Clarrie Grimmett and Bill O'Reilly (who dismissed Hammond ten times in Tests) and they found a way to expose his relative weakness on the leg side; even if he scored runs, they made sure he scored them more slowly than before. It is hard to tell to what extent he also suffered from the presence in the opposition of Bradman – whose 974 runs in just seven innings in the 1930 series obliterated Hammond's 1928–29 record – but it was undeniably the case that if England were to compete with Australia on a regular basis they needed runs from their star performer. From 1930 onwards, Hammond outscored Bradman in only five of the 27 Tests in which they opposed each other – and in one of those Bradman was injured and did not bat.

But it would be easy to overstate these problems. Hammond added three more centuries in Australia to the four he scored there on his first tour, the last of them a match-winning 231 not out at Sydney in 1936–37, while his 240 at Lord's in 1938 saw him at his majestic best.

Nor did he reserve his best for international cricket. He maintained a remarkably high standard in county cricket as well, dominating the national batting averages throughout the 1930s and regularly finishing among the leading catchers. That said, he perhaps touched a peak in 1928 during his first home summer as an England cricketer when in all first-class cricket he scored 2,825 runs, took 84 wickets and held 78 catches; during Cheltenham Week in August he scored 139 and 143 and took ten catches against Surrey before following up with 80 runs and 15 wickets (nine for 23 in the first innings) against Worcestershire. Neither his catches for the season nor his catches in the match against Surrey have ever been beaten by an outfielder.

Of the seven batsmen who have topped 50,000 first-class runs, Hammond's average of 56.10 is clearly the highest, Herbert Sutcliffe standing next on 52.02, while only Hobbs and Patsy Hendren have managed more first-class hundreds than Hammond's 167. His 819 catches put him fourth on the all-time list among non-keepers. He took 732 first-class wickets at an average of 30.58. As an all-rounder, he stands second only to Garry Sobers.

7. JACK HOBBS

England 1907–30

There is no more persuasive testimony than that of one's peers, and Jack Hobbs's teammates and opponents were united in their admiration and praise. They rated him as the best of all batsmen. His technique was regarded as immaculate and in an era when the ultimate test was how someone coped on rain-affected pitches – the infamous 'sticky dog' – he was regarded as the master. Famously, he and his protégé Herbert Sutcliffe both scored hundreds in nightmarish batting conditions at The Oval in 1926 to set up a victory that ensured the Ashes were regained after a long wait, and the two of them also coped brilliantly in similarly treacherous circumstances – the ball rising around their heads and shoulders – at Melbourne in 1929 to set up England's biggest successful run-chase, a performance all the more extraordinary because Hobbs was by then 46 years old. Age clearly had not withered him. In the final match of the same series, which spanned an incredible 33 days, games in Australia then being played to a finish, he scored 142 out of England's first 235 runs; no one else has ever scored a Test match hundred at such an advanced stage of life. Some critics, noting 'The Don's' reluctance to come to terms with batting on 'sticky dogs', rated Hobbs even higher than Bradman himself.

Hobbs was also the first batsman to really conquer the new googly bowlers that emerged in Test cricket in the first decade of the 20th century. He scored 539 runs in his first Test series against South Africa, who had the best array of googly bowlers including Bert Vogler and Aubrey Faulkner, averaging 67.37, double the figure of the next best player on the England side. The next winter he scored 662 runs in five Tests against Herbert Hordern, Australia's new googly sensation. He was also superb against the extreme pace of Jack Gregory and Ted McDonald who destroyed England shortly after the First World War, proving an impeccable judge of which balls could be left. In Australia in 1920–21, he averaged 50.50 when no other England batsman topped 40.

When he retired from Test cricket in 1930, the Australian players stopped the game at The Oval to give him three cheers, the first time they had done that. If the Aussies are prepared to do that, you must be good. And why wouldn't they? Hobbs's record against them was exceptional: 3,636 runs and 12 hundreds. Even today, no one from any country has ever done better. He was the first batsman to score 5,000 runs in all Test cricket and his average of 56.94 has still been beaten by only a select few. 'Hobbs was the greatest English batsman I've seen and tried to remove,' said RC Robertson-Glasgow, who played for Somerset for many years and was later a distinguished cricket correspondent. 'He was the most perfectly equipped by art and temperament for any style of innings on any sort of wicket against any quality of opposition.' Quite apart from his ability, he was by all accounts an outstanding sportsman who played the game in the right spirit. Little wonder that he was knighted, the first professional cricketer to be so honoured.

It was not just his record against Australia that stands out. His first-class records of 61,237 runs and 197 hundreds are both records that will never be beaten. Like Sachin Tendulkar in a later era, not the least remarkable aspect to him was that the appetite for the game never seemed to dim. Hobbs was not only fit enough to score 100 hundreds after his 40th birthday, and keep batting into his 50s, he remained for a long time a very athletic fielder who was still patrolling the covers effectively enough in his late 30s – and in the heat of Australia at that – for his opponents to agree a pact: 'No runs to Hobbs'. There surely cannot have been a better outfielder to that point.

Probably like most professionals of his era, Hobbs was motivated largely by the need to earn a decent living and provide for his wife and four children. In his case there appeared to be the added incentive of making sure that they escaped the poverty in which he had grown up. Born and bred in extremely modest circumstances in Cambridge, the eldest of 12 children to a father who sometimes worked as a groundsman and umpire, he himself worked in a variety of menial jobs before being persuaded by Tom Hayward, one of the finest cricketers in the country and an inspirational figure to the young Jack, to try his luck at The Oval. Hobbs, who received little formal coaching, was 22 before playing

his first full season of county cricket but made an immediate impact, scoring 88 in his first match and 155 in his second, which included 137 before lunch. As such a performance suggested, Hobbs was a highly attacking batsman, something he remained until war interrupted his career in 1914. This was quite unusual for professional batsmen of the time precisely because their livelihoods depended on them not failing, but Hobbs was good enough to back himself to come out on top, as he often did. The game as a whole became more cautious after the war and Hobbs said he did not like the obsession with statistics during this period (he would often give away his wicket after reaching his hundred) and preferred the carefree approach of his earlier days.

One statistic did matter to Hobbs, or at least it was one statistic that he could not escape. In 1925, he attracted frenzied national interest by surpassing WG Grace's tally of 126 centuries, but such was the fuss in the build-up that he lost form horribly for six matches before drawing level with Grace and then going past him in the same game against Somerset at Taunton. His poise recovered, he finished the season with 16 centuries, itself a record until Denis Compton beat it in 1947.

Some felt that Hobbs might have been England's first professional captain of the 20th century had he pushed harder for it. In fact, he was entrusted with leading the team on to the field during a Test against Australia at Old Trafford in 1926 when the official captain, the amateur Arthur Carr, was unwell, and that same year Hobbs and Wilfred Rhodes became the first professionals to sit on the selection panel. But Hobbs was too nice a man to agitate for such a revolutionary step and the English game had to wait until Len Hutton in the 1950s for the change to be made.

6. BRIAN LARA

West Indies 1990–2007

Sachin Tendulkar's international career may have been half as long again as Brian Lara's but Lara arguably played more truly brilliant innings that took the breath away with their technical mastery and audacity. Lara was capable on his day of shredding even the finest bowlers in a way that few if any of his peers could match. He won games off his own bat, something that convinced some of his superiority to Tendulkar. What is beyond argument is that for many years these two incredible cricketers – Lara at 5ft 8in the taller by three inches – stood head and shoulders above their batting rivals.

Lara will be best remembered for twice claiming the world Test record score – the 400 not out against England in Antigua in 2004 still stands – and his 501 not out for Warwickshire in a county championship match against Durham, which remains the highest individual innings in any first-class match. Astonishing though these displays were in their scope and stamina, as was his original Test record score of 375 in 1994, also against England in Antigua, he had even better days than those.

What marked him out was how he dealt with the best bowlers of his day. He was absolutely brilliant against Muttiah Muralitharan in Sri Lanka, and that is not easy. Nor was this someone thinking in terms of taking ones and twos, and of rotating the strike, and boring the bowler to death. He was picking each delivery, and whacking it, and making Murali the Magnificent look Murali the Mortal. He was every bit as good against Shane Warne. Only eight Test double-

centuries were scored against Warne and Lara scored three of them. One of these came in Jamaica during a remarkable series in 1999 which was drawn 2–2 and went through every conceivable twist and turn. In the previous game West Indies had been dismissed for 51, leaving Lara's future as captain on the line. A match-winning 213 was his response. He then played even better in the next game in Barbados, carrying his side to an improbable victory with an unbeaten 153 after his team lost their eighth wicket with 63 still needed. Curtly Ambrose and Courtney Walsh in turn held firm but of necessity Lara did most of the scoring. Warne suffered the rare indignity of being dropped for the next match.

Lara must have been one of the best of all time against spinners. Perhaps he was fortunate to be brought up in Trinidad (as the tenth of 11 children) where pitches turned more than elsewhere in the Caribbean. Even so, the way he dominated Murali and Warne was very special.

He was also, it seems trite to say, very good against pace, at least until his later years when a tendency to jump across his crease became exaggerated and he was perhaps grateful for the protection the helmet afforded him. His first international hundreds came against world-class fast bowlers such as Wasim Akram and Waqar Younis for Pakistan and Allan Donald for South Africa while playing as a one-day opener in 1993 when they were at something like their peaks. It is surprising to think that Lara did not score his first century for West Indies until he was 24 years old but despite the obvious excitement over his ability in his native Trinidad, where in his second match for the island he scored 92 against a Barbados attack containing Marshall and Garner, and his own immense self-belief, he was kept waiting for his chances. He had played only two Tests by the time he turned 23 but in his first full series scored 277 at the SCG, an innings that not only turned the series but many heads too. Lara described it as his favourite innings and named his first child Sydney in its memory. I was commentating for Australia's Channel Nine during that match and can testify to Lara's brilliance.

The difference between Lara and so many of the other batsmen in this list was the strength of the team he was playing for. For the most part it was not great (and sometimes downright terrible). West Indies relied on him so much. Lara finished on the losing side in almost half of all the Tests he played – 63 out of 131 to be precise – but the blame could not often be laid at his door. He scored 5,316 runs in those 63 defeats at an average of 42.19 with 14 hundreds. Lara sometimes enabled West Indies to compete with the stronger sides, but often the challenge proved too much even for him. In his greatest series against Murali in Sri Lanka in 2001, Lara scored a staggering 688 runs in three games, yet all three games were still lost. When he played for Warwickshire in 1994, he helped turn a modestly talented team into treble-winners.

The 400 not out, which came in the fourth and final Test of a series, was shaped by three earlier defeats. In the context of the game, it was perhaps overdoing it, but given what had happened in the series, it was his way of restoring pride in West Indian cricket and salving the wounds inflicted by Michael Vaughan's pace attack, against which he personally had had to grit his teeth and battle hard. I was there as a broadcaster for that innings as I had been for the 375 ten years earlier. On the first occasion there was something really romantic and emotional about watching Garry Sobers, one of my great heroes and Lara's too, walk out to congratulate him. Sobers said he could not have been happier that Lara had been the one to break his record:

'To me he is the only batsman around today who plays the game the way it should be played. He doesn't use his pads, he uses his bat.' I'd interviewed him at the start of the 2004 series and asked if there was a chance of him reclaiming the record and he'd said, 'Oh well, maybe, you never know. I'm not really thinking about it ...'

Perhaps most extraordinary was how relaxed he was when he resumed on 313 at the start of the third day. As part of Sky TV's build-up, we were on the outfield and we'd asked him if we could borrow his bat. I was holding it and saying, 'This is the bat with which Brian Lara is today going to attempt to get back his world record ...' And then there he was, walking past on his way to the wicket. 'Here you are, you might need this ...' He said thanks and off he went to get his 400. Most players would have wanted that bat with them in the dressing-room, familiarising themselves with how it felt again. Not Lara. He had far too much style for that.

Did he get a little bit carried away with himself at times? Possibly. There perhaps was one difference with Tendulkar. When he suddenly became very famous he found it hard to handle the change in lifestyle and it took him time to adjust. Nor did the West Indies captaincy always sit easily with him.

His technique was far from orthodox. He had a high backlift, which made him vulnerable to fast yorkers if he was not in the right position, but conversely it meant his hands were high for the cross-bat shots at which he excelled, and it helped generate tremendous bat speed and therefore tremendous power. Denying him width was the best way to keep him quiet, as Glenn McGrath showed, but few had McGrath's discipline. By and large his quick eyes, hands and feet allowed him to get into good positions and make outrageously late adjustments to his shots. There were repeated rumours, towards the end, that his eyes were going, but if true they did not stop him playing until his 38th year, scoring a double century in his penultimate Test, or retiring with more Test runs to his name than any other cricketer to that point. Of course, Tendulkar overtook him in the end.

5. VIV RICHARDS

West Indies, 1974–91

Of all the batsmen I played against in Test cricket, Viv Richards was the one you most feared would take the game away from you. He possessed a magnificent physique and a powerful personality, and was highly driven by a fierce pride in being among the first Antiguans to represent West Indies, his close friend Andy Roberts having beaten him to the honour by a matter of months. At a time when few West Indies cricketers had emerged from outside the main islands, they both knew there was something special about that. Later, when he took over the West Indies captaincy from Clive Lloyd, it was pride again that spurred him to build on the good work done by his predecessor and make sure the team maintained their pre-eminence.

Viv quickly gained a fearsome reputation as a batsman, scoring 192 in his second Test match away to India before putting together a string of big scores in his annus mirabilis of 1976, which he began by making runs against Lillee and Thomson in Australia as an opener – he later settled in the pivotal number 3 position behind Gordon Greenidge and Desmond Haynes – and crowned with an astonishing series in England in which he plundered 829 runs in four matches, including a glorious 291 at The Oval. That was his personal response to Tony Greig's ill-advised prediction that England might make West Indies 'grovel'. People learnt to choose their words carefully when Viv was in the opposition.

I'd come up against him on a handful of occasions in county cricket before, but the first time I really experienced the full impact of his batting was in the World Cup final of 1979 when he played an innings of absolute brilliance, aided and abetted by Collis King. We had West Indies in some trouble before those two got together and we rather ran out of bowling! We just couldn't separate them, at least, not until it was too late, Viv finishing with 138 not out. There were to be a few more days like that, some of them when I was captain and charged with setting fields to a man who could be impossible to contain. The most extreme example of that came in a one-day international at Old Trafford in 1984, the first meeting of the sides that summer.

On that occasion we had them in even greater trouble at 166 for nine. What followed was a masterclass both in batting and in how to manage a difficult situation, with Viv manipulating the strike in order to keep his partner – Michael Holding – out of trouble. Viv was toying with me: wherever I put the fielders seemed to make no difference and during the last 14 overs of the innings that they stayed together Viv faced all but 27 balls and scored 93 of the 106 runs they put on. It was much the same two years later when he scored what was then the fastest Test hundred in history off 56 balls in his beloved Antigua (it has since been equalled, by Pakistan's Misbah-ul-Haq, but not beaten). He simple took the mickey. If I put the field out, he would run two; if I brought it in, he would hit the ball over the top for four or six. It was unbelievable, godlike stuff.

Viv had a very distinctive style. Everyone thought they had

a chance if they bowled straight at him because he liked to play across his front pad and work the ball to leg. Bowlers were sure he'd miss one, but he seldom did. The power was the other thing that struck you. He wasn't particularly tall at 5ft 10in, but he had the shoulders of a boxer.

He never seemed intimidated by anyone or anything, even if he got hit, as occasionally he did in the Caribbean playing inter-island matches. He took the blows but never showed the pain and certainly never admitted to it. His decision to never wear a helmet – during a period when every other player in the game wore one as a matter of course – was an audacious statement of superiority and one he never had reason to regret. Even at the age of 38, playing in the championship for Glamorgan against Hampshire, his eye was good enough for him to take 14 off the last over from Malcolm Marshall – four, six, four – to win a game we thought we'd had in the bag. Going into the last hour Glamorgan, five wickets down, still needed 112 to win and we thought Viv had miscalculated: fat chance. He took particular pride in launching vendetta-like assaults on the best fast bowler in an attack, as Bob Willis discovered to his cost during the 1980 series in England.

Viv learnt a lot from the mauling West Indies suffered at the hands of Lillee and Thomson in Australia in 1975–76, where they lost five of the six Tests, but also from World Series, which is where he would have had some of his severest tests. In 14 World Series 'Supertests' he scored 1,281 runs at an average of 55.69, a record that none except Greg Chappell and Barry Richards could remotely match. In official Test cricket, his return was 8,540 runs and 24 hundreds, and at the time he was chaired off the field having drawn the 1991 series in England 2–2 to ensure he maintained his record of never losing a series as captain, only two batsmen had scored more runs in Tests and only three had made more hundreds.

Whether or not he was actually captain, Viv embraced the role of leader, both within his team and in the wider sense of representing the people of the Caribbean. The West Indian community may not have heaped expectation on his shoulders in quite the same way as the Indian population did with Sachin Tendulkar, but nevertheless a lot of hope was invested in his performances and he rarely let his public down. In fact, he improved pretty much every team he played for, including Somerset (whom he helped win their first trophies, before the relationship soured and he was controversially sacked), the Leeward Islands, Queensland and Glamorgan.

Occasionally, his pride spilled over into odd territory, with him once failing to lead out his West Indies team because he had gone to the press box to harangue an English journalist about something he had written, but he was by and large a principled man with a fiercely competitive streak. There was so much more to him than simply his batting – captaincy, useful off-spin bowling and brilliant fielding, initially in the covers, later at slip. The first time many people were aware of him was when he executed three brilliant run-outs during the 1975 World Cup final. He remains the only West Indian to score 100 hundreds in first-class cricket.

4. SHANE WARNE

Australia 1991–2007

Shane Warne changed the culture of the game. After an era dominated by fast bowlers, he arrived on the scene at just the right time to exploit the minds of batsmen armed with helmets, heavy bats and back-foot techniques designed to counter a battery of pace-men. Abdul Qadir had been the only spinner who regularly won matches for his country and he was only really effective at home in Pakistan. Warne proved dangerous across the world. He revived the art of spin bowling to a global audience just as satellite TV was bringing the game into their living rooms. Plenty of spin bowlers who have subsequently played Test cricket since said they were inspired by watching him. He made spin bowling as sexy as it could be.

There was so much to the overall Warne package that it is easy to forget just how phenomenal his gifts were. In his early years, he had the ability to bowl huge leg-breaks but also managed to get them to swerve through the air: this was what really did for Mike Gatting at Old Trafford in 1993 with the 'Ball of the Century'. The swerve drew Gatting over to the leg side before the ball had pitched; once it hit the turf, it spun sharply away towards his exposed off stump. He also possessed a lethal flipper. His googly was not reckoned to be that good by the highest standards, but it hardly needed to be. As the years took their toll, and surgery was required on shoulder and fingers, the power of these physical weapons diminished but he more than made up for it with his cunning and intelligence. He had an amazing talent for working out a pitch, and an opponent, within a few deliveries.

He developed a body language and a kidology that were all his own. He had an 'aura' and it did for many an unsuspecting foe and quite a few suspecting ones too. He proved to be so much more than just a little fat kid from Melbourne who liked junk food and failed in his first ambition to be an Aussie Rules player. The pressure built on the batsmen as the Warne legend gained momentum from the Gatting Ball, the hat-trick in Melbourne, the Chanderpaul Ball at Sydney

in 1996 and the Strauss Ball at Edgbaston in 2005. Australia's amazing win over England at Adelaide in 2006 owed much to him. It was Warne who mesmerised everyone, including the umpire who gave out Strauss to a dodgy decision to start the collapse on the final morning. He had the confidence to try things others dare not, and to persuade others to believe, like him, that the impossible could be done.

He also set batsmen up in a way that I think was extraordinary. In a recent documentary on Sky he revealed how he had bamboozled Alec Stewart in the first Test of England's first tour to Australia during the Warne era. He served Stewart a ball that was short and wide, giving him the chance to cut – giving him, in effect, a four, not something I realised that any bowler was prepared to do! Then he gave him something similar but subtly different. Stewart again shapes to cut, only to realise too late that he's been done: it's the Warne flipper and it bowls him. I'd not seen that from a bowler before and it was not something I understood. I'd been brought up in county cricket and with England to think that bowlers were not in the business of giving you things.

Little wonder few dared take risks against him. This made him very different from your average leg-spinner. Growing up playing the game in England, I like many others did not see that much leg-spin. That came on tours, especially of Australia where even in the pace-centric 1980s there would usually be one in each state side. Most of them were capable of bowling magic balls with the extra turn that comes from good wrist spin but you knew that they would relieve the pressure with the occasional 'four' ball when they got it wrong. In that era Pakistan's Abdul Qadir was easily the best I faced: he had good variety and good disguise, and I loved the challenge. The difference with Warne, whom I missed by a whisker (maybe thankfully), was that he gave away next to nothing – unless he wanted to do as part of a larger plan! If need be he was actually a great defensive weapon. No more could a leg-spinner be brushed off as an expensive luxury.

Even Sachin Tendulkar said he could never relax when facing Warne. It is revealing that the only regular batsmen who averaged 50 in Tests against Warne were Tendulkar (60.45), Brian Lara (55.57) and Kevin Pietersen (53.50), none of whom could be remotely described as ordinary performers; nor could VVS Laxman, who dealt with him brilliantly. It took something special to succeed against Warne.

Although Muttiah Muralitharan's Test record is superior, many leading batsmen who faced both were in no doubt that Warne was the superior operator, essentially for the reason that Tendulkar gave – that he never let them (or, it might be added, the umpires, whom he worked relentlessly) relax. Second best his statistics may be, but they are still astonishing: 708 wickets in 145 Tests at an average of 25.41. He took 195 wickets in 36 Tests against England alone: no bowler has ever taken more against one country.

Of course, he did have one big advantage for much of his career, which was playing in a side as strong as Australia. Every spin bowler needs runs to play with and Australia routinely piled up the big scores that gave him the canvas to work with and made his job much easier. If Australia batted first, which they almost always did to allow Warne to bowl last, their opponents were often chasing daunting totals in the fourth innings that they were never likely to get (only once in 36 times did Australia lose with Warne in their side when defending more than 315 in the fourth innings; only three other times were they denied victory). That said, there are great pressures on a spinner to finish the job in the fourth innings, and it was a pressure Warne dealt with brilliantly. Nor could it be said that he had runs to play with at Adelaide in 2006 and he still came up trumps. Which other spinners might have won the game that day?

Warne's talents did not end with his bowling. He was a superb slip catcher and a useful lower-order batsman capable of making a serious nuisance of himself, as he repeatedly showed during the epic 2005 Ashes series when he scored 249 runs as well as taking 40 wickets. He had an instinctive understanding of the game and a superb tactical awareness and would have made an excellent and fascinating captain of Australia had the authorities trusted him beyond a few one-day internationals. That they did not must be a lasting regret for him but perhaps he had only himself to blame for his one-year drugs ban in 2003 and his off-field escapades that put him on the front pages as well as the back, and cost him the support of large swathes of the Australian public. His private life was often turbulent and never dull but the more trouble he seemed to be in, the better he appeared to play on the field.

3. SACHIN TENDULKAR

India 1989–2013

It is ridiculous to recall that I actually played Test cricket with Sachin Tendulkar. I retired what feels like a long time ago – it was a long time ago – and yet throughout the intervening period, at least up to late 2013 when he finally bowed out amid great fanfare in his home city of Mumbai, the little master continued to play the game at the highest level and, for the most part, to an amazingly high standard.

When I faced him in England in 1990, he was a mere 17 years old but even then was astonishingly good. He had first played for India the previous year and had shown resolve on a tour of Pakistan, but we were privileged to see an early glimpse of just how good he was when he saved the Old Trafford Test with an unbeaten hundred. He also took an astonishing one-handed running catch to dismiss Allan Lamb at Lord's when I was at the non-striker's end. He still says it was the best catch he ever took.

Two years later he was scoring hundreds against Australia in Sydney and Perth, the latter a ground where visiting batsmen traditionally struggle with the pace and bounce. If anyone can be described as a cricketing prodigy, it must be him.

During their schooldays, some reckoned that Vinod Kambli was actually the better player, which only goes to show that the key to greatness is not just raw talent but having the right mindset. There is no doubt that Tendulkar had that. In fact, it was precisely that mental strength and determination, that relentless appetite for the game, that saw him keep going for so long, pushing past one milestone after another, so that by the time he retired his record stood as not only unmatched but probably uncatchable: 200 Test matches, 15,921 Test runs, 51 Test hundreds; 463 one-day internationals, 18,426 one-day runs, 49 one-day hundreds. All are records and all evidence of sustained excellence in all conditions.

Like Sunil Gavaskar, another in a long line of prolific run-scorers to come out of Mumbai, he was very small at 5ft 5in and very nimble. He was rarely caught out of position for any shot. He had an unusually low grip on the bat, and a surprisingly heavy bat, which helped him generate power, but his overall technique was immaculate. He was a master technician and an absolute genius.

The World Cup final of 2011, when India beat Sri Lanka in Mumbai, was not his night in terms of what he contributed to the game but everyone in the India team that night instinctively said, 'We've done this for Sachin'. It was his sixth World Cup and the first he had won and it seemed only fitting that he should be a victor at least once. He was such a humble, modest, quietly spoken man. He had none of the swagger of a Viv Richards, or the flamboyance of a Brian Lara, although you wouldn't say he lacked confidence. He was always very contained and very controlled, and you can only be that controlled if you have huge confidence and huge ability. He exuded an air that said, 'You are never going to get me out', and that in itself must have been intimidating.

Had things been slightly different he might have retired straight after that World Cup triumph on home soil but his legion of fans would never have allowed him to quit with 99 international hundreds to his name, which is what he had at that point. Rather bizarrely, it took him almost a year to add that one extra but all-important hundred to his list, as for once even he felt the pressure of expectation. His game suffered during that period and in truth his form was pretty ordinary during the last couple of years of his career, but that was probably the only time that could be said of him. He had suffered dips before but there was usually an explanation, such as a serious tennis elbow problem that hampered him around 2005–06. Just when people started to wonder whether he was on the wane he had an astonishing year in 2010, when he turned 37, scoring seven Test hundreds and becoming the first in history to score a double century in a one-day international.

It is worth noting too that among that century of international centuries 20 were scored against Australia, who for much of the time that he was playing were the best team in the world and possessed two all-time great bowlers in Shane Warne and Glenn McGrath. Warne said no one played him better.

With a billion Indians hanging on his every move, he played under ridiculous pressure of a kind that none of us can understand. The expectations were unrealistic yet he somehow managed to leave his audience satisfied. There was a real dignity to everything that he did and considering how long he played it was extraordinary how rarely he put a foot wrong or caused offence with something he said. He probably experienced his most difficult times during two relatively short stints as India captain, which did not work out well for him. Generally speaking though, with one exception when he was cited in a ball-tampering row in South Africa, which in turn led to the most ridiculous political posturing from the Indian management, his was a career free of controversy, and how many can say that?

One accusation was that he did not always win as many matches for India as he should have done; that there were of course lots of runs and plenty of meaningful contributions from him, but not many match-defining efforts for a performer of his stature. There was probably some truth in this claim, although only some. He won countless one-day internationals for India, especially in the 1990s when he was in his pomp as an attacking opening batsman in the 50-overs format and he would have walked into anybody's one-day World XI. There was more of a case to answer in Test cricket, although he was hindered for a long time by India's lack of strength in bowling which meant they found it hard to drive home winning positions. Even so, it is surprising to learn that he was man of the match only five times in Tests that India won.

This, of course, was what added extra spice to the wonderful century he scored on a worn pitch to win the Chennai

Test against England in 2008 when India as a nation was recovering from the terrorist attacks in Tendulkar's native Mumbai. England had held the upper hand for much of the game and when they set India 387 to win must have been confident that they could pull off what would have been a famous victory, given that winning in India is something that they have never found easy to do. Tendulkar's innings that day put the smiles back on the faces of a nation and proved that he could see his side home even in the most difficult circumstances. Ironically, that was not one of the games in which he was named man of the match – Virender Sehwag took the award for a whirlwind 83 that launched the run-chase. But it is a game that everyone now remembers as 'Tendulkar's match'.

Apart from all those extraordinary statistics, I think that his sheer love of the game and appetite for playing it are what mark him above his potential rivals for the accolade of the finest batsman of the modern era. To maintain such stratospheric standards for so long is simply remarkable. His status as a demigod in Indian cricket circles is assured for all time.

2. GARRY SOBERS

West Indies 1954–74

I have to declare an interest. Garry was and remains a hero of mine. I have vivid memories from my childhood of going to Trent Bridge to watch him play for Nottinghamshire and thinking, wow, this guy is special. All the Sobers hallmarks were there: standing absolutely dead still at the crease, minimal foot movement, great follow-through, the ball ricocheting off the boundary boards as not a man moved. The way he moved was magical; a lithe, lissom, loose-limbed creature. Just to be able to carry off the whole thing must have been a triumph. I also remember the famous film of his epic innings for a World XI against Australia at the MCG at New Year in 1972, 254 of the finest runs you will ever see, a genius at work against some of the best bowlers in the world. It was described by Bradman as 'probably the greatest exhibition of batting ever seen in Australia'.

Garry was the supreme all-rounder, an almost mythical figure who could bat, bowl quick, bowl swing, bowl cutters, bowl spin, catch pigeons, play golf and of course famously carouse. You would not recommend to a young player today all aspects of his self-confessed love of life – the gambling has obviously been a bit of an issue for him – but I remember him saying that if he was a little bit late of a night he felt he owed his teammates a good performance the next day, so perhaps that side of things did not do his game any harm. His 26th and last Test century against England at Lord's in 1973 was apparently scored after a night on the tiles.

In contrast to today's hard-headed world where winning and stats are everything, there was a certain romance about the way he played to entertain. Of course, this did not always work out to his advantage – there was that infamous declaration against England in Port of Spain in March 1968, which cost West Indies the match and ultimately the series – but the game as a whole was better for it. It was entirely appropriate that he should be the first man in the history of the first-class game to hit six sixes in an over, on 31 August 1968. I recall watching the footage of that on the BBC in *Grandstand* the following Saturday. My father was livid

because I forgot to call him through to be able to see it too!

Has there been a more versatile or natural cricketer? His status as the greatest ever Test all-rounder is rarely if ever questioned. Jacques Kallis's figures bear comparison but Sobers was more of a front-line bowler and more capable of winning a match. For most of his career he would have been worth picking as batsman or bowler. There was nothing negative about his play. He didn't use pad-play and he 'walked' if he knew he was out. Bradman said he saw no one hit the ball harder. He was largely untroubled by the best and fastest bowlers of his day – Ray Lindwall, Keith Miller, Fred Trueman, you name them – and even in an era before helmets he wasn't in the habit of being hit on the hands or the body.

He was largely uncoached. Born in humble circumstances in Barbados, he was brought up as one of seven children by his widowed mother, his father having been killed in the war while serving on a merchantman that was torpedoed in 1942. Even so, he was playing for West Indies by the age of 17, chosen initially as a left-arm spinner who batted low in the order; just four years later, having moved up to number 3, he was breaking the world Test record by scoring an unbeaten 365 against Pakistan at Kingston, Jamaica. True, the bowling was not the toughest, but then nor had he previously scored a hundred for West Indies. When his record eventually fell, to Brian Lara in Antigua in 1994, Garry was on hand to witness the handing over of the baton to his young protégé.

It is hard to imagine that he could ever have played differently to the way he did, but he was profoundly affected by the death of his West Indies teammate Collie Smith in a car accident in 1959 when Sobers was at the wheel. 'In all my innings, I played with him inside me,' Sobers said.

These days, cricketers are used to the idea of playing all the year round, but it was less common before air travel made the world a smaller place. Garry was among the earliest jet-age players and throughout his pomp he maintained an amazingly full schedule. He played domestically with great success in England for Lancashire League teams, and later for Nottinghamshire, and for South Australia in the Sheffield Shield, all the while continuing to perform for Barbados and West Indies. Of course, his body felt the burden in the end, but he was naturally fit and amazingly did not miss a Test match between 1955 and 1972.

His record against England was astonishing. In 36 Tests against them, he scored 3,214 runs at an average of 60.64 and took 102 wickets at 32.57, as well as 40 catches that he would have taken with minimum effort. His performances in the 1966 series in England must rank among the finest of all time: 722 runs, 20 wickets and 10 catches. But he also averaged more with the bat than the ball – which has always been one of the best measures of an all-rounder's worth – against both Australia and India.

At the time of his retirement in 1975 – the year he was knighted – his career tally of 8,032 runs in official Tests had not been bettered but that haul takes no account of the many runs he also scored in matches for the Rest of the World against England in 1970 and Australia in 1971–72 that ranked as Tests in all but name. Indeed, for several years the England matches counted in the Test records before being reclassified on the insistence of the game's rulers.

His regrets must be that he missed out on the riches the modern game has had to offer – imagine how much he would fetch in an IPL auction – and that, after taking over from Worrell, West Indies did not really progress under his captaincy, although he was hardly the only great player for whom leadership did not work out. He had little enthusiasm for the politics that motivated many West Indies players, some of whom he disappointed by visiting Rhodesia and not criticising the Caribbean rebels that toured apartheid South Africa.

1. DON BRADMAN

Australia, 1928–48

His figures and feats are ones with which you simply cannot argue. Indeed, his record is so far ahead of anyone else's that one can scarcely believe one man could be so dominant through a career spanning 20 years. Whereas most players, if not every other player but him, went through dips in form, he maintained his supremacy each year, every year. That was what really set him apart. As Wally Hammond said, Bradman's whole career demonstrated his merciless will to win. One can only admire the mental strength he must have possessed.

As with WG Grace, it often became a match between the opposition and him. 'He spoilt the game,' Jack Hobbs said. 'He got too many runs.' Australia lost only two series in which he played. Both were against England. The first was in 1928–29 when Bradman was appearing for the first time and was dropped for one game after making an innocuous debut (his response when he was recalled was to score two hundreds in the remaining three games). The second came in 1932–33 when Douglas Jardine deployed his infamous Bodyline tactics. That series represented Bradman's most serious failure and yet he averaged 56.57: that's not failure in other people's books. These were the only two series in which he averaged less than 70.

I've seen brief glimpses of footage of him batting and wondered about some of the field settings, which hardly seemed designed to slow down the scoring. He himself has conceded that the game in those days was in some respects very different from the way it later became. When Shane Warne and Sachin Tendulkar were granted an audience with him in the 1990s, an interesting conversation ensued in which 'The Don' was asked how he might have fared in the modern era. He said he would not have scored so many runs precisely because of defensive fields; in his day, fields remained attacking for far longer, even when batsmen were scoring quite freely. There was no such thing as a deep point or sweeper in those days and he also conceded that the standard of fielding was much better in the modern game. His admission that he might have averaged nearer 70 than 100 had he played in the modern era prompted some jokes along the lines of 'Not bad for a 90-year-old', but his comment was probably a serious and revealing one.

To an extent, the transformation in fielding standards helps to explain one of Bradman's key strengths, which was the phenomenal speed of his scoring. His two Test triple-centuries were both scored in matches in England restricted to four days: in the first one in 1930, he scored 309 of his 334 runs in one day, including a hundred in each of the three sessions. In that series, consisting of four matches lasting four days and one (the last one) played to a finish, he scored 8, 131, 254, 1, 14, 334 and 232 for an aggregate of 974 which still stands as the record for any series, even though many series since have been played over more matches and more days.

That innings of 334 was at the time the highest ever played in a Test match and meant that he held the records in both Test and first-class cricket, having earlier that year scored an unbeaten 452 (in just under seven hours) for New South Wales against Queensland in Sydney. He was just 21 years old at the time. His personal view was that his innings of 254, made in the second Test at Lord's, was the best of his career.

For him, though, scoring fast did not mean taking foolish risks. His method was so clinical and efficient – if not always pretty enough for some purists – that he hit few sixes and rarely hit the ball in the air (he had an unorthodox grip that did not lend itself to aerial shots). And even if we concede that the standard of fielding was not as high then as it is now: it was the same for everyone in his time and he still stood head, shoulders and a fair bit of the body above his peers in terms of productivity.

He was clearly an interesting character. Talk to the likes of Ian Chappell, who knew The Don pretty well, and what comes back is not all sweetness and light. He appears to have been prickly and critics will call him self-centred and self-interested. It was pretty well known at the time that Bradman did not see eye to eye with several other Australian players, the Irish-Australians Bill O'Reilly and Jack Fingleton among them. When Australia – without Bradman, who was recovering from illness – happily toured South Africa under Vic Richardson in 1935–36, only for Bradman to be appointed captain in his place for the following winter's series against England, it was not a popular decision with all parts of the dressing room. But Bradman proved as ruthless and as successful a captain as he was a batsman, and the results brooked little argument. A classic example of his leadership style came in that 1936–37 series against England when he reversed his batting order on a rain-affected wicket so that by the time he went in, at number 7, conditions had improved and he was able to score what proved to be a match-winning 270.

His contribution went beyond just the playing feats. He also had a role in management and was a very influential member of the Australian board. Some feel he might have done more to see that players were better remunerated in the period leading up to their decision to take Kerry Packer's dollars, but he also played an undeniably beneficial role in eradicating 'chucking' and in encouraging the teams to play enterprising cricket ahead of the famous 1960–61 series between Australia and West Indies. With a similar ambition in mind he was also instrumental in Garry Sobers, the world's biggest drawcard, joining South Australia the following year.

I met him briefly once in Adelaide on one of my early tours, a chance encounter walking round from the dressing rooms to the dining room. I was struck by how small he was, a reminder that many of the finest batsmen – Sachin Tendulkar, Brian Lara and Sunil Gavaskar also come to mind – are not great hulks. He was 5ft 8in tall and not powerfully built. You imagine that when you meet such a revered figure there will be a golden aura surrounding them, a great charge of energy when you shake hands, and pearls dropping from his lips when he speaks. In reality he exuded coolness, calmness and a normality that hid the great ability and determination. One of the first cricket books I ever read, and pored over, was his masterly *Art of Cricket*.

While it is hard to compare different societies and different times, Bradman carried the hopes of a nation on his shoulders, just as Tendulkar did for Indians in a later era. In Bradman's case, Australians were feeling acutely the consequences of the First World War, which had left their relationship with Britain under strain, as well as the Great Depression. Sport gave them an identity and Bradman provided them with their most reliable champion. But the burden took its toll, which only makes his achievements all the more remarkable.

Bradman himself said that his concentration was what set him apart from others. He was famously single-minded in practice as a child, using a single stump to hit a golf ball against a water tank outside the family home in Bowral in rural New South Wales where he grew up, the fifth child of a wool trader and carpenter. He was 17 years old when he made scores of 234 and 300 for Bowral, the former against a young O'Reilly (off whose bowling he was dropped twice before reaching 50). This led to an invitation to attend a practice session at the Sydney Cricket Ground, and ultimately to an offer to play for the St George club. In his first match for them – and his first-ever match on a turf wicket – he scored 110. A little more than a year later he was playing his first match for New South Wales and scoring another hundred.

What was particularly striking was how Bradman was equal to each and every new challenge that was presented to him. He made a success of his first season of state cricket and his first season as a Test cricketer, despite being dropped after one game. When doubts were expressed that he would struggle in English conditions on his first tour in 1930 his response was to hit 236 at Worcester in his first match and he went on to make 1,000 runs before the end of May. Such indeed were his powers of concentration that he was never out in the 90s in Test cricket (he scored 29 hundreds).

He was certainly fortunate to play in an era tailor-made for batsmen. Scoring in state cricket in Australia was huge and before Bradman had arrived on the scene Bill Ponsford twice played innings in excess of 400. Far fewer Test matches were played in those days but even so three other batsmen besides him made Test scores of more than 300 in the 1930s. In the series in which Bradman made his debut, Wally Hammond topped 900 runs. Bradman therefore had plenty to aim at in terms. Just how well he succeeded can be measured by a first-class career average of 95.14 and career Test average of 99.94, which remain well ahead of all his rivals. He played at a time when big scores – massive scores – were a necessity, and he provided them like no batsman before or since.

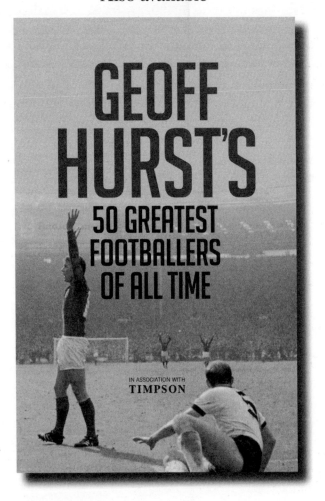